BETTER BOSS BLUEPRINT

HOW GREAT MANAGERS BUILD TRUST, INSPIRE LOYALTY, AND DELIVER RESULTS

DR. KATE VAWTER

For permissions requests, write to info@betterbossblueprint.com.

Quantity Sales. Special discounts are available on quantity purchases by nonprofits, corporations, associations, and other entities. For details, contact info@betterbossblueprint.com.

The web addresses referenced in this book were live and correct at the time of the book's publication, but may be subject to change.

The advice and strategies found within may not be suitable for every situation. This work is sold with the understanding that neither the author nor the publisher is responsible for the results accrued from the advice in this book.

Cover design by: Kate Vawter

Library of Congress Control Number: 2025920823

Printed in the United States of America

Paperback ISBN: 979-8-9931813-1-8
Hardback ISBN: 979-8-9931813-2-5
ebook ISBN: 979-8-9931813-0-1

Shalimar Business Press

To my LEADing ladies and Class 30 family.

Table of Contents

Introduction:
Human-Centered Leadership

Many new managers are often handed the mantra, "I'm not here to be their friend," as if it's a requirement for credibility. It comes from outdated leadership models that teach distance is the same as authority. But that approach doesn't hold up in today's workplace, and in truth, it never really did.

Strong leadership doesn't come from keeping people at arm's length. It comes from showing up with presence, building connections, and creating a space where trust can grow. When your team knows you see them, hear them, and respect them, they're far more likely to rise to the occasion.

Let's rewind for a moment. If you are already a manager, I want you to think back to when you first got your promotion. You were probably a rock star in your previous role, nailing every task, every project. And then— *bam!*—you're a manager. Now you're in charge of people, and if you're like most, you were given little to no guidance on what comes next.

A lack of support often sets the stage for accidental toxic leadership. Most bad bosses aren't intentionally difficult; they are trying to navigate uncharted waters without the tools they need. The fear of messing up, combined with the stress of not knowing what to do, creates insecurity and frustration. Those emotions, left unchecked, can quickly snowball into micromanagement, poor communication, or a detached leadership style. It's a vicious cycle: the more a manager struggles, the harder it is to connect with their team, and the more disconnected they become, the worse things get.

We in corporate America are constantly frustrated with leadership. Bad bosses are so common they've become a punchline. Think about all the comedy shows, movies, and books dedicated to terrible management. It's a trope at this point! But while we love to laugh at what a boss shouldn't be, we rarely talk about what a great boss should be.

The root of this issue is a lack of manager training. Most organizations don't invest in preparing people for leadership. They don't teach the skills needed to manage effectively or even how to handle the day-to-day realities of leadership. The result creates talented, well-meaning people who are thrown into leadership roles and expected to figure it out as they go. And let's face it, when you're in over your head, it's nearly impossible to lead with confidence or clarity.

On top of that, there's a stigma around how we believe we are expected to manage. Many new leaders feel like they need to emulate the tough, distant bosses they've seen before. There's this fear that being approachable or empathetic might undermine authority or invite slacking. But that's not how people work. People aren't lazy when they are healthy and cared for. Actually, they are wildly productive.

So, how do we fix this? How do we become the leaders our teams need us to be with very little training and support? That's what this book is all about. We'll start by tackling the common struggles new managers face. Whether it's feeling unsupported, grappling with fears of failure, or navigating the discomfort of new responsibilities, the transition into leadership can be daunting. This book will help you understand those challenges and, more importantly, give you the tools to overcome them.

From there, we'll dive into strategies you can use right away. Want to have better conversations with your team? We've got you. Need to figure out how to balance being supportive without losing authority? That's here too. We'll talk about the different hats managers wear, when to put them on, and how to use them effectively. We'll explore trauma-informed management and how to help your team navigate big feelings, even when you're dealing with your own. And for the days when you're just trying to survive? Don't worry, there's a plan for that too.

I have been in your shoes. My leadership journey started early, from student roles to managing million-dollar budgets and overseeing teams of dozens (sometimes hundreds) of people. I've had to figure out how to lead during massive organizational changes, how to communicate expectations without killing morale, and how to build relationships that keep things running smoothly. I've seen what works, what doesn't, and why prioritizing people over process is the secret to success.

Which is why I became a leadership coach and started Ascent Solutions. My goal is to help new leaders like you master human-centered leadership that drives results. And let me tell you, when you get this right, it's like flipping on a light switch in a dark room. It just works. Suddenly, your team is *thriving*. They are catching problems before they explode into full-blown crises, and they're bringing you solutions. When you invest in your people, they trust you. And when they trust you, they're willing to take risks, grow into bigger roles, and stick around longer. Plus, let's be honest, it's way more fun to work somewhere where people actually like and support each other. Organizations that put relationships first are more successful[1] and they are places people actually want to show up on a Monday morning. Imagine that.

This book isn't here to hand you a magic formula or tell you there's one "right" way to do this. Though "blueprint" is in the title, it's here to give you options, ideas, and the tools you need to figure out what works for you. Because at the end of the day, great management isn't about being perfect. It's about being present, being real, and being willing to learn as you go.

As you read on, you'll learn how to:

- Build connections that make communication easier and more effective.
- Navigate the balancing act of leadership.
- Create a culture where people feel safe to grow, share, and thrive.
- Handle tough conversations with grace and confidence.
- Reflect on your own journey and use it to become the leader you were meant to be.
- What hats you should wear as a manager (and when to swap them out).

---

[1] (Beechly, 2022)

Finally, I want you to remember two things. First, you don't need to know everything to be a good leader. Second, you can be a friend *and* a manager. It is possible. I'll show you the tools you need. Don't leave your personality at the door and assume you must put on a mask when you lead others. The most successful leaders are the ones who show up as their authentic selves, who care about their people, and who are willing to learn along the way.

My goal is to help you feel confident in your ability to effectively support your team. Bring your willingness to grow, and I'll bring the tools to help you get there.

Chapter 1:
The Support Struggle

Many managers are thrown into leadership with little more than a "Good luck!" and a link to the HR portal. It's no wonder so many of us quickly become burned out. Support shouldn't be a luxury, but often, that's exactly what it is.

The first time I found myself managing people without a roadmap was during my time as an undergraduate student at a large state university that shall remain unnamed. The department I led managed student events with a team of thirty people, most of whom were also students. I was twenty years old and facing a tough job made tougher by the shifting workforce. Every couple of years, half the team would move on, graduating into the next phase of their lives. That constant turnover meant I was always hiring, training, and scrambling to maintain momentum. And somehow, in the middle of all that, I still had to build a culture where people could work together without clashing.

I was a student myself, wholly responsible for all of my finances, and this managing role was a part-time stipend position that barely covered the hours I worked, let alone the stress it came with. Had I done the math, I probably would've discovered I was only making a few dollars an hour, if that. This definitely wasn't enough to cover my bills. So, on top of schooling and this stipend position, I had to get a second part-time job. The balance was grueling. I often found myself working fifteen-hour days. My pink beach cruiser bike became my daily constant, ferrying me between classes, the office, and events, before taking me home just to do it all again the next day.

Yet, managing this department remained my top priority. Even when I knew it wouldn't pay my bills, I cared deeply about the work we were doing. The events we planned were moments of belonging for our peers and a source of pride for the university. Failure wasn't an option. If an event was poorly executed, everyone saw it. I didn't want that to be our brand. I believed in our mission, in the value of our work, and in the importance of doing it well.

Budget management was another mountain to climb. Managing a million-dollar budget as a student from a low-income background was daunting. Every dollar spent required my signature, and it felt like the weight of the world rested on those pieces of paper. I wanted to ensure every cent of my peers' money was spent responsibly.

I worried constantly—would we pull this off? Would we make a good impression? Would our work reflect the passion and effort we put into it? Every detail mattered. For many, including me, these events were a lifeline. A break from the relentless pressure of classes and life challenges. They mattered deeply to me because I saw firsthand how much they mattered to my peers. That sense of purpose, of knowing the work made a difference, pushed me through the exhaustion and the uncertainty.

But the reality was relentless. There was no downtime and no slowing down. The work was a constant stream of demands, and the problems I faced felt overwhelming, especially for someone in their early twenties. Nobody trained me to be a manager. There was no roadmap and no handbook for managing emotions, navigating difficult decisions, or keeping a team aligned. And, perhaps worse, there was no one to turn to for guidance.

Then I had to fire someone for the first time. I remember to this day the knot that formed in my stomach when I realized what I had to do. The guilt and shame overwhelmed me. It was the right decision, but that didn't make it any less gut-wrenching. I had no experience to guide me—just a sense that it needed to be done. With no training or resources, it was a trial by fire. I did it, reflected, and hoped to do better next time.

Managing people, projects, and finances all at once—without training—was isolating, nerve-wracking, and a crash course in leadership I hadn't realized I signed up for. One day I was a peer, the next I was a manager, juggling new expectations without meaningful feedback or support. To make matters worse, the one advisor I did have turned out to be less than trustworthy.

I had hoped he could be a mentor, someone to rely on when I didn't have answers. But that illusion shattered soon after I turned twenty-one. He invited me to have a drink and met me at Applebee's that afternoon. Then, once he had swallowed a particularly large and fruity margarita, he leaned across the table and said, "I don't understand why we can't be together."

Gross, right? Did I mention he had a girlfriend at the time?

I was floored. Here was someone I thought I could trust, someone who should have been supporting me, and he crossed a line I couldn't ignore. I reported the incident through every available channel—emails, formal reports, and direct conversations—but nothing changed. Each time, I was met with dismissiveness or silence, leaving me feeling unheard and powerless. I pushed harder, going up the chain of command, hoping to find someone who would take the situation seriously, but the inaction was deafening.

Despite my efforts, no one intervened. I was left to continue managing the team with him as our advisor while navigating my complicated emotions and carefully ensuring no other women on the team had to interact with him alone. It felt like walking on eggshells. And I consistently questioned if I had done something wrong, all while trying to maintain a professional facade in an environment that felt increasingly unsafe.

While many of you might not be facing this exact situation (at least, I hope you're not), the management learning curve is steep. Too many of us don't have the support we need, or the support assigned to us simply isn't present. And the safety net is practically nonexistent.

New managers are often left fumbling their way through tricky situations, without a mentor to offer a lifeline or a support system to fall back on. It's like being asked to assemble IKEA furniture without instructions. Sure, you might get there eventually, but not without a lot of stress and a few extra screws leftover. This lack of guidance piles on the pressure, leaving many managers wondering if they're even cut out for the role.

Leadership by Fire Hose

Many organizations promote individuals because they are good at task-oriented work without equipping them for leadership-oriented work. This is the core of the support struggle.

Too often, people who excel at individual tasks and show care for their organizations find themselves suddenly elevated into management positions. But being great at tasks doesn't automatically translate into being prepared to lead people, manage projects, or oversee budgets. In fact, it might not even reflect a *desire* to do those things. The transition is jarring. You go from being a colleague and having work friends to being a manager where the dynamics shift entirely.

Adding to the challenge is the lack of validation. Middle management often exists in a feedback void, where consistent communication about performance is scarce. Senior leaders assume you're fine because you are not the one causing problems, and direct reports aren't in a position to tell you what's working, so no one does—leaving you to steer the ship without a compass, hoping you're headed in the right direction.

Without regular positive reinforcement, it's easy to feel like you're constantly falling short, even when you're not. That feeling only gets worse in workplaces where competition quietly overrides collaboration. When peers are fighting over resources, decisions are made behind closed doors, and everyone's guarding their turf, management can feel like a lonely place to stand. In these environments, a rising tide doesn't lift all boats; instead, it leaves people scrambling not to be thrown off the ship entirely.

Navigating this minefield requires skills many new managers haven't had the chance to develop: self-validation, confidence, and the ability to recognize their own wins, plus the ability to put on different hats at different times, knowing how to use those hats. Without mentors to illuminate the path or the support of a healthy organizational culture, the journey can feel disorienting. The American cultural expectation of "you're a manager now, figure it out" compounds the problem, setting new managers up for a trial by fire that I find unnecessarily painful.

In my work with clients, I see a consistent need for support. You might already feel like something's not working, but you can't quite put your finger on why. That uncertainty isn't a personal failing, it's a symptom of stepping into leadership without a blueprint. That's why I name the struggles here, clearly and directly. Because once you can see the problem, you can start to solve it. Let's take a closer look at the most common internal and external challenges new managers face.

Common External Struggles

Stepping into leadership means shifting from doing the work to directing it. You are no longer focused on tasks; you're making decisions, setting priorities, and managing people. It's an entirely different kind of responsibility and uses different brain power. Because of this transition, there are a few key external struggles you will likely run into as a new manager. Each one presents its own unique hurdles, and understanding these can make navigating them less daunting.

Decision-Making Fatigue

Transitioning from task execution to decision-making is one of the most jarring shifts for new managers. Before, you could focus on crossing items off your to-do list, but now every move you make requires deliberation, strategy, and foresight. Decisions require more cognitive energy than repetitive tasks, and it doesn't take long for your mental reserve to drain.

On top of that, there's the constant question: Should I involve the team in this decision, or is this something I should decide alone? While making a quick decision might seem easier (and frankly faster), it can sometimes undermine long-term success. Excluding your team from the decision-making process can chip away at their intrinsic motivation. But involving them too much can slow things down and lead to decision paralysis. Finding the balance is tough, and frameworks like the Eisenhower Matrix or a weighted decision matrix can help, but these tools require practice. For new managers, it's a steep learning curve, and it can feel like every choice you make is being scrutinized.

Personally, I like using a weighted decision matrix framework.[2] Start by identifying the key variables for the decision (things like budget, time, and how it will impact customers and staff). Assign a value to each variable to show its importance. Then, come up with realistic options. Include a "do nothing" option as a baseline (Option A) and add a couple of actionable paths (Options B and C). Assign scores or "low-high" ratings to each variable for every

---

[2] (Scholz, 2023)

option and sum them up to get a clearer picture of the best course of action.

Below is an example of how this might look when considering whether a business should hire an outside consultant or manage the project themselves when switching their HR platform.

This method helps you think through the decision strategically and provides a transparent way to present your rationale to the team or leadership. It's a simple, structured approach that ensures you're weighing the factors that matter most, and it can save your brainpower for the next big decision on your plate.

	Financial Cost	Time Cost	Impact on Staff
Do Nothing	Low	Low	High
Hire Consulting Team	Very High	Low	Low
Manage Project In-House	Moderate	High	Moderate

Providing Feedback

For the most part, new managers think their role is to tell people what they did wrong. I disagree. The job of a manager is to tell people what they have done well.

In American culture, it's all too common to go weeks—or even months—without hearing a simple acknowledgment of a job well done from our boss. And while we've normalized this, it's far from healthy. Exceptional managers consistently acknowledge the strengths and accomplishments of their team members. But this doesn't come naturally to most of us. Many of us didn't grow up in environments where consistent praise was part of daily life, and learning how to give positive feedback is a skill. Like any skill, it requires practice.

That said, not all praise is created equal. Simply saying, "Good job," isn't enough. Truly impactful feedback is specific, thoughtful, and intentional. Expanding the phrase into, "Well done handling that client with professionalism and empathy," makes a world of difference. And while constructive feedback is important, I firmly believe that positive feedback should always take precedence. As managers, we should create a safe space for open, honest conversations about growth and improvement, focusing on desired outcomes rather than fixating on mistakes.

For instance, instead of saying, "This missed the mark" or "You failed at this" (which is never appropriate feedback), I prefer to sit down with team members and collaboratively explore what they might want to approach differently next time. This approach reinforces trust and mutual respect. We are all adults, we know when we have done something wrong or a project didn't go well. We don't need it pointed out to us. Instead, a conversation rooted in shared goals and ideas for next time is much more productive.

Implementing Change

Change can come from different directions. Sometimes, it's a policy or directive handed down from executive leadership. Other times, change is driven by our own initiatives as new managers looking to improve our teams or processes. How we approach these changes—

especially when they may not be well-received—can define our effectiveness as leaders.

When executive leadership imposes a policy change, we often do not agree with it. However, our role is to communicate these changes in a way that is thoughtful, strategic, and empathetic. Consider a difficult scenario like a decision to withhold cost-of-living wage increases due to financial challenges. While leadership delivers the decision to you, it's your responsibility to pass it on to your team.

This is not the time for a group announcement. Instead, this bad news should be a one-on-one conversation. It allows you to connect with each individual, acknowledge the difficulty of the news, and emphasize your advocacy for them. Let them know you see their efforts and value their contributions. If possible, reassure them that you'll continue to advocate for their needs when resources allow. Addressing this one on one instead of in a group setting allows you to create a space where each team member feels safe to react or respond. For some, this news might have serious personal implications, and they need to know you're there to support them, even if that means assisting them with finding opportunities elsewhere. Delivering hard news with understanding and care shows leadership beyond the policy itself.

On the other hand, when the change comes from us as new managers, we often make the mistake of rushing to overhaul processes or structures in an effort to prove our value. It's tempting to think that initiating sweeping change signals leadership, or that you should make changes because you were promoted to do so, but implementing change in isolation is rarely successful. If we dictate changes without input, we risk alienating the team, damaging morale, and undermining our own credibility.

Instead, approach change as a collaborative effort. Start by defining the problem with your team. Invite their perspectives, insights, and ideas, and work together to develop a solution. When everyone has a hand in shaping the new path, they're far more likely to support it and implement it wholeheartedly. It positions you as a leader who listens and values the expertise of your team, rather than someone who simply dictates terms from above. This is how we create sustainable change that lasts long after we've discussed it.

Turnover and Training

For many new managers, turnover feels like a personal failure. But let me assure you it's not. Turnover is a normal, healthy part of any organization. People grow and change as the circumstances of their lives evolve, and that's natural. Turnover is a reminder that every individual's journey is unique, and the organization will continue to thrive as people move through it.

That said, effective hiring and a strong training program can help mitigate the impact of turnover. When we prepare our teams well and cross train on work, the departure of one member doesn't leave the department in disarray. Creating redundancy is key to handling turnover with grace. This ensures that if someone leaves, their responsibilities don't fall through the cracks, and you aren't blindsided and hurrying to try and train someone else on what they do. It allows you to accept the resignation with understanding and empathy instead of frustration and worry.

Training, however, is often misunderstood. Many new managers expect a quick learning curve for new hires, only to be frustrated when the process takes longer than two weeks. This frustration is normal, but it's important to remember that learning curves vary widely. Everyone absorbs information at their own pace, and proficiency takes time. Before you were a manager, you were likely very fast at a task-driven job. It's often part of why you became a manager! But that speed will not be the same for everyone.

Successful training is a long-term investment. While initial orientation might last two weeks, truly mastering the role often takes closer to a year. During this time, in addition to learning the tasks required for the work, new employees are also learning the culture, politics, and language of the organization. This includes understanding how to communicate effectively, such as crafting the appropriate tone in emails to different audiences or navigating the nuances of internal processes. These skills are as critical as the tasks themselves, but they take time and repetition to develop.

As a manager, you will need to practice patience and recognize that excellence doesn't happen overnight. Folks won't be wizards in two weeks, or even two months. Sure, they might have gone through the orientation training or been introduced to the procedures. But they need time to gain confidence, adapt to the organization's rhythms, and understand the subtleties of their role. This timeline includes experiencing a full cycle of seasonal or annual processes, which often reveal the more intricate aspects of the job. Mastery requires time. But with the right training and support, your team members will grow into their roles.

We all face the bubbling sense of urgency triggered by the external pressures of leadership. Keep in mind that these pressures can push you to react in ways that aren't healthy for us or our team. And it only gets worse when internal struggles start whispering, "You're not cut out for this," right when you need confidence most. My favorite tactic? Reminding myself I don't save babies. It's not that urgent, and it's not that serious.

If that one doesn't do it for you, don't worry, next we'll take a closer look at the internal struggles you'll face and how to overcome them next.

Common Internal Struggles

The scariest part of stepping into a management role isn't the endless meetings or the surprise budget reviews. It's the nagging little fears that sneak in when you least expect them, whispering all sorts of unhelpful nonsense like, "You're doing it wrong," or "Everyone's judging you." These fears are universal, but luckily, they are conquerable. Let's break them down one by one.

Impostor Gremlins

Have you ever wondered if your leadership team picked the wrong person? Or maybe they gave you the job because no one else wanted it? Welcome to the club. Impostor syndrome is like a loud, annoying coworker who keeps telling you you're not good enough, and spoiler alert: they're lying.

Brené Brown calls these "anxiety gremlins," and they show up at the worst times. Whether it's the "manager gremlin" whispering that you're not qualified or the "money gremlin" insisting you can't handle a budget, their goal is to make you doubt yourself. And while these feelings are valid, they are also bullshit.

As Carol Dweck teaches us in her book *Mindset*, when we have a mindset that with time and energy we can learn to do anything, we find success.[3] Adopting this way of thinking allows us to believe more in other people and in ourselves. The next time that gremlin shows up uninvited, remind yourself you weren't promoted by accident. Someone saw your potential and believed in you, so why shouldn't you? You may not know how to do something at this moment, and that's okay. Being willing to learn will help you shut down these gremlins.

Sky-High Expectations

It's easy to feel like senior leadership is sitting in a secret room somewhere, measuring your every move against an impossible standard. I promise you, they're not.

In fact, that pressure usually doesn't come from them. It comes from you agonizing over how that email sounded, second-guessing your decision in yesterday's meeting, or replaying a one-on-one conversation on loop in your head. Most of that pressure is self-imposed and isn't grounded in reality.

If leadership had doubts about your abilities, you wouldn't be in this position. They selected you for this role because you are a capable individual, not because they wanted to set you up for failure. Pause and question these fears. What evidence is there that expectations are

---

[3] (Dweck, 2007)

unreasonably high? Most of the time, these perceived pressures don't exist. The real challenge lies in overcoming our own internal narratives and focusing on the work at hand. If this is really resonating with you, recommend checking out Martin Seligman's work, such at *Learned Optimism.*

Grounding yourself in fact is the antidote to this pressure. By letting go of unattainable standards and trusting in your ability to rise to the occasion, you create space for growth, progress, and confidence. Meeting real expectations, and often exceeding them, is about showing up, learning as you go, and staying focused on doing the job well.

Social Isolation

I can't tell you how many times clients have told me, "Now that I'm a manager, I can't have any friends at work." And while this is also a valid feeling, it is also bullshit.

To lead well, you need people in your corner. Full stop.

You need trusted relationships where you can be real, ask hard questions, and admit when you don't know what you're doing. You need allies you can vent to without fear and brainstorm with when you're stuck.

That kind of support doesn't have to come from someone on your team, or even inside your organization. It could be a peer at another company, a former supervisor, or someone else who understands your world. The point is, you can't do this alone, and you don't have to.

Ideally, you want to find people in your organization who are on the same level as you or above you in the organizational structure. The first will give you comradery and community, the second will give you understanding of the bigger picture and how to walk the line. They may say, "Yeah, that challenge sucks, but it's normal, and it's not actually up to you to solve." This will help you move forward with confidence! They can help you see what is and isn't within your realm of control.

When you surround yourself with the right people, you create a space to be human in a role that often expects you to be superhuman. That support system can be the difference between constantly second-guessing yourself and moving forward with grounded confidence. So, before you convince yourself that leadership has to be lonely, take a beat. Find your people. You don't have to approach leadership without backup.

Doing It Wrong

Nobody nails everything on the first try. You're going to make mistakes. Yet, making a mistake is one of the most paralyzing fears for new managers. Whether it's mishandling a budget, making a poor hiring decision, or staying silent in a room filled with organizational powerhouses, without a clear blueprint, the fear of doing it wrong can be overwhelming.

In larger organizations, this fear is often amplified by the sheer number of meetings and the weighty topics being discussed. It's easy to feel like your contributions aren't enough, or worse, that staying quiet might signal you're out of your depth. But this fear is a healthy sign that you care about doing your job well.

Mistakes, whether big or small, are part of the human experience. No one enters a new role with all the answers, and perfection isn't a realistic expectation for you, your team, or your work. What matters is how you handle those moments of imperfection. Use them as opportunities to learn, reflect, and adjust.

Rather than aiming for perfection, strive for what I call "good enoughness." Excellence is a worthy target, but you will have to do a lot wrong before you hit the bullseye. Building time for reflection and feedback into your team's routine allows you to make steady progress towards excellence.

That can look like literally saying aloud to your team, "We are going to mess things up sometimes, and that's okay. We will debrief, so we can figure out how to do it better next time." Then creating a system of debriefs worked into your team meetings or project wrap-ups. The more you practice owning your missteps with curiosity instead of shame, the more resilient and respected you become as a leader.

Being Disliked

Ah, the classic worry: "What if they don't like me?" Some managers lean into this fear and become people-pleasers; others go the opposite direction and decide they don't care at all. Neither approach works. One leads to burnout and frustration, while the other builds walls that isolate you from your team.

To lead authentically, focus on self-awareness and personal growth. Understanding who you are, what you value, and how you want to show up in the world provides the foundation for confident leadership. Your worth shouldn't rest solely on your identity as a manager. It should be spread across the many roles that make up who you are—a parent, a friend, an artist, a mentor, or, in my case, a dog mom and a baker. When your self-worth is grounded in multiple areas, negative feedback in one doesn't shake your entire foundation.

The fear of being disliked often stems from a deeper place, and addressing it may require intentional effort. Whether that's through counseling, diving into self-help resources, or even binge-watching insightful YouTube content, taking the time to understand why this fear exists is a worthy investment. It's a more deeply rooted challenge than others and deserves the energy required to untangle it.

At the end of the day, showing up as your authentic, thoughtful self is what matters most. And yes, some people won't like you. That's a fact of life, and a reflection of them, not you. By focusing on your values, you can lead with confidence, even when not everyone is on board. The goal isn't to be universally liked, but to be genuinely respected for who you are and how you lead.

Lean into the Chaos

At the end of the day, these internal and external struggles are part of the messy, beautiful journey of being a manager (and a human). They'll show up uninvited, but they don't have to stick around. Recognize them, confront them, and keep moving forward. *Lean into the chaos.*

Many managers are out there winging it, navigating obstacles and fears without a blueprint or support system. Maybe even your manager. Being thrown into leadership without guidance is like being handed the keys to a car you've never driven and told to win a race. You'll figure it out, but it might get messy. Luckily management isn't about having all the answers.

Chapter 2:

Discomfort Is Normal

Think of fear and comfort as points on a spectrum that every leader moves through repeatedly. On one end, you've got the comfort zone (warm socks, coffee in hand, no surprises) where everything feels safe and familiar. You know the routines, and things are low stakes.

Take a step outside that zone, and you enter the fear zone. This is where things start to feel shaky. Doubt creeps in, and your inner voices get loud. It's uncomfortable, but it's also where change starts. The trick is not to get stuck here. If you push through that fear, you'll find yourself in the learning zone. Here, the discomfort is still present, but so is growth. You start trying new things, getting feedback, and building confidence bit by bit.

Eventually, if you keep going, you'll hit the growth zone. This is where things click. You begin to trust yourself, challenges feel exciting instead of paralyzing, and the scary stuff starts to feel doable. Which brings you right back to the comfort zone.

This cycle (comfort, fear, learning, growth) is the rhythm of leadership. Each time you level up, a new comfort zone forms, and a new edge appears. The goal isn't to avoid discomfort, but to learn how to walk through it. It is totally normal to feel uncomfortable when learning something new. Researchers have coined this the Dunning-Kruger Effect. When we first learn something new, it feels like we suddenly know it all. As we learn more, that shifts to feeling like we know nothing. As time passes, our knowledge continues to increase, as does our confidence.

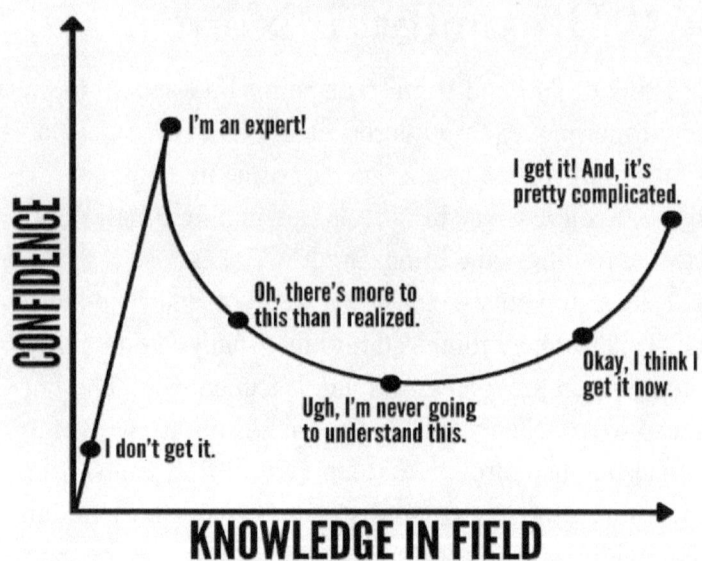

One of my clients is a coffee shop manager who started as a part-time barista with solid coffee and customer service skills. She knew her way around a latte art heart and could chat with customers like a pro. Then, boom!—she got tapped for a leadership role. Cue the fear zone. Suddenly, she was tasked with things she'd never done before, including managing people, creating policies, and having tough conversations. Her gremlins had showed up in full force!

But she said yes to the role because her life vision is to own a coffee shop someday. So, she knew she had to take this step, even if it felt like stepping off a cliff. My job was to help her minimize the fear and embrace the learning zone instead. Through my coaching and support from the owner, she began to tackle the challenges one by one. She learned how to give feedback, communicate clearly, and, most importantly, believe in herself. The fear zone didn't magically disappear—it never does—but it got quieter. Now, she recognizes discomfort for what it is: a normal part of growth.

As leaders, I can promise you we will be uncomfortable. And, on top of our discomfort, those on our team will periodically be uncomfortable. You might have recently been promoted to the role, but now your direct report who has been working in their role for a few years has to adjust to reporting to you. I can guarantee they will feel uncomfortable too. They will wonder: *What does this person know that I don't? Will they respect my experience? Will things change now that they're in charge?* Discomfort is a shared experience in leadership, but it's also a sign of growth.

In her book *Danger in the Comfort Zone*, Judith Bardwick, says, "We know that productivity suffers when uncertainty is high. But we've failed to realize the equally destructive effects of too little anxiety. By protecting people from risk, we destroy their self-esteem. We rob them of the opportunity to become strong, competent people."[4] Let that sink in. Staying in the comfort zone feels safe, but it also means staying stuck.

As a manager, your job isn't only to nudge yourself out of that warm, fuzzy cocoon—it's to give your team a gentle (but firm) shove out of theirs, too. Growth doesn't happen in the safety of what's familiar. It happens when you stumble into the fear zone.

---

[4] (Bardwick, 1995)

The SCARF Model

When it comes to discomfort, you can't just slap on a brave face and hope for the best. You need tools to navigate it, both for yourself and your team. The SCARF Model can help. Developed by David Rock, this framework is rooted in neuroscience and aligns beautifully with human motivation theory.[5] This model is all about creating an environment where people feel ready to tackle the big stuff. SCARF—an acronym for Status, Certainty, Autonomy, Relatedness, and Fairness—hits all the psychological sweet spots, so you and your team can grow without spiraling into stress naps and existential dread. Let's break it down.

Status

Whether you perceive your power or not, as the manager, you have it. Think of it like inheriting a lightsaber—you might not feel like a Jedi yet, but everyone else sees you holding the thing and assumes you know how to use it. As humans, we're deeply attuned to status. It affects how we interact with others and shapes the dynamics of every workplace. For new leaders, this can be one of the hardest adjustments to make. One day, you're part of the crew, swapping memes and venting about work; the next, you're "The Boss," and suddenly your casual suggestions sound like official decrees. It's weird, and it takes time to figure out how to wield that influence without accidentally killing the team's morale.

It might feel to you as if nothing has changed when you get promoted. That you are still "one of the group," but your direct reports no longer see you that way. They see

---

[5] (Rock, n.d.)

your status. You have authority over their livelihoods. You hold the power to give raises, assign projects, or even make tough decisions like terminations. This power shifts how people hear and interpret your words. A casual comment from you might carry far more weight than you intended, and your team's reactions might surprise you.

Denying or ignoring your status doesn't make it go away. It leaves you wandering through leadership like someone who accidentally became king but refuses to wear the crown. Whether you acknowledge it or not, your words carry more weight now. If you don't recognize that power, you risk sending mixed signals, making people second-guess themselves, or fostering resentment from a team that feels unheard or undervalued.

Instead of pretending nothing has changed, embrace your status in a way that benefits your team. Think of yourself as someone who clears the path, removes obstacles, and helps others step into their own potential. Use your influence to build trust, amplify voices, and create opportunities. Recognize the privilege that comes with your role and wield it with care.

This might look like calling out someone publicly[6] in a team meeting when they have consistently delivered outstanding results. You might say, "I want to shout out to Shereen for her incredible work on the new client onboarding project. Her attention to detail and commitment

---

[6] Before publicly recognizing someone, it's nice to check in with them that they are comfortable with that. Personally, I hate public recognition. Other recognition options could include a handwritten thank you note, an email to your boss singing Shereen's praises and bcc-ing her on it so she can see it or bringing in her favorite morning beverage and saying thank you one on one.

to the timeline have been a game-changer for our success."
By acknowledging Shereen's status as a high-performing
contributor, you validate her efforts and inspire others to
aim for similar recognition.

Certainty

We humans are creatures of habit. We thrive on
routine, predictability, and the assurance that we know
what's coming next. Certainty provides a psychological
anchor. It keeps us calm, focused, and motivated. When
that anchor is shaken, discomfort sets in, and fear takes
over. As a leader, your job is to provide as much certainty
as possible, even in uncertain times.

The early days of the COVID-19 pandemic were a
perfect storm of uncertainty. Businesses didn't know
whether they would stay open, teams were unsure if they
would keep their jobs, and leaders were scrambling to adapt
to new realities. In moments like these, clear
communication is your most powerful tool.

Reassuring statements like, *"Your job is secure,"* or
"Our company is stable and moving forward," can go a
long way in calming fears. Even if you don't have all the
answers, sharing what you do know creates a sense of
stability for your direct reports.

On the flip side, failing to provide certainty can have
spectacularly disastrous effects, kind of like yelling "Don't
panic!" in a crowded room and watching everyone
immediately panic.

One client I worked with ran a small organization of
about twenty employees. During a stressful quarter, she
started walking around casually dropping comments like,
"If sales don't improve, I'll have to lay everyone off." She

didn't actually mean it. She thought she was lighting a fire under her team, giving them a wake-up call to push harder. But when people hear the word "layoff," they don't feel motivated. They think about eviction notices and buying groceries. Instead of doubling down on their work, her employees likely spent more time updating their résumés and whispering in break rooms about job security. You can bet morale took a nosedive and productivity plummeted, and instead of a high-performing team, she had a room full of stress-induced zombies counting down the days until the inevitable.

Uncertainty breeds fear, and fear isn't a great motivator—it's a paralyzer. If you want your team to perform well, give them stability. Even in tough situations, clarity and honesty go further than empty threats or vague doom-and-gloom statements.

If your team is facing a period of uncertainty, like a reorganization, a shift in company strategy, or a sudden departure of your beloved CEO, instead of leaving them in the dark, overcommunicate what you do know. Hold a town hall meeting and address the team directly, saying, *"I know this transition is stressful, but here's what I can tell you. No one's job is in jeopardy, and our goal is to come out of this stronger as an organization. We'll share updates weekly, and I'm always available to answer your questions."*

Sadly, most managers will say something like, "Big changes are coming, and I can't say anything yet." While that statement may be true, it doesn't provide any clarity. The former statement is equally true, and it helps the team know they shouldn't be worried. Lack of clarity frustrates people. Instead, lean into transparency wherever possible, even if you don't have all the answers. The more certainty someone has, the safer they will feel, and the better their performance will be.

Autonomy

Autonomy is the sense of control one has over their decisions, tasks, and environment. It's a fundamental driver of motivation. When people feel they have the freedom to make choices, they're more creative and productive. Many new managers worry giving autonomy means taking your hands off the reins, but that isn't what you are doing at all. This doesn't mean chaos or letting your team run wild like kids in a candy store. It's about giving them the right amount of freedom and providing a clear framework while trusting them to make decisions within it.

As a leader, your job isn't to micromanage every move—it's to set the stage. Be crystal clear about your organization's vision, values, and goals. Paint a picture of what success looks like, outline the guardrails, and then (this is the hard part) step back. Give your team ownership. Let them take the wheel, make choices, and learn from them. When people feel trusted, they rise to the occasion. And when they don't? Well, that's a coaching opportunity, not an excuse to yank back control. (We will dive into how to wear the coaching hat well in coming chapters.)

If people don't understand the "why" behind their tasks, they're less likely to feel motivated or aligned with your goals. What's more, they are more likely to do the wrong thing, simply because they didn't understand what was needed. When that happens, that poor performance is actually on you as the manager, not them.

After setting the vision and expectations, step back and let your team take ownership of the process. Trust them to assign roles, set deadlines, and problem-solve without micromanagement. Of course, you can check in periodically to offer support, but resist the urge to overstep. There's close to a zero percent chance that anyone else will do the work exactly as you would have, but that doesn't mean they won't achieve the desired outcome. Even if you think you might need to get involved in the process, pause and ask yourself if you actually need to intervene or if you're just annoyed something isn't going the way you pictured it. This balance of autonomy and guidance empowers your team to feel in control and motivated to deliver. Like other management skills, you'll likely feel a bit uncomfortable when you first try it, but with practice and patience, you will see how much autonomy strengthens your team.

Relatedness

At our core, humans are social creatures. We need connection, belonging, and trust to feel comfortable and motivated. This is where relatedness comes in. It's about building relationships that foster collaboration and mutual respect.

Trust doesn't magically appear just because you all share an office (or a Zoom link). It must be built, brick by brick, through consistent actions. One way to kickstart this process is by creating opportunities for low-risk vulnerability.

To help with this, I developed a game called *"I'm Glad You Asked,"*[7] designed to help teams build trust incrementally. The game includes questions at varying levels of vulnerability, from light and fun (*"What's your favorite snack?"*) to more personal (*"What's a challenge you've overcome recently?"*). Pulling one card per week at team meetings can spark meaningful conversations and help people connect on a deeper level.

The goal of this game is to lay down a foundation of trust. Every positive interaction, every kind word, every moment of listening adds to this foundation. Eventually, those small moments add up, giving your team something solid to stand on when things get tough.

Keep in mind this shouldn't be the only way you build trust. You also need to build trust with cultivated consistent actions over time. Start with small, meaningful gestures. For instance, if you're leading a remote team, begin meetings with a quick personal check-in: *"What's one good thing that happened to you this week?"* This creates space for connection and helps the team bond on a human level. If an employee shares a personal challenge, take time to listen and empathize. A quick, sincere *"I'm here if you need anything"* can mean the world to someone navigating a tough time.

Your team isn't a collection of job titles. They're a group of real humans, with real lives, real challenges, and real dreams, all working together toward something bigger than the next deadline or KPI. When you strip away the org chart and the email signatures, what you have is a group of people who, on any given day, are balancing workloads,

---

[7] (Vawter, n.d.)

personal struggles, ambitions, and the occasional existential crisis about whether they left the garage open.

You don't work with "Marketing Coordinator, Chelsea." You work with Chelsea, who is brilliant at brainstorming ideas and gets nervous about presenting in big meetings. You don't manage "Operations Specialist, Paola." You manage Paola, who keeps things running smoothly but is secretly worried about balancing work and grad school. When you take the time to see the humans behind the roles, you create an environment where people feel valued for who they are.

When people feel seen, they show up differently. They collaborate better. They take risks. They bring their full, engaged selves to work. They don't do the bare minimum to keep their job and quiet quit their way to a paycheck; they lean in. That's what relatedness is all about. It's the difference between a workplace that feels transactional—"I do the work, you pay me, we go home"—and a workplace that feels connected.

Fairness

People have an *uncanny* ability to detect when the scales aren't balanced, it's practically a sixth sense. The moment they perceive favoritism, inequity, or bias, trust starts eroding, morale dips, resentment brews, and suddenly, you've got a team more focused on who's getting what than doing great work.

If one person consistently lands the best projects, the most desirable shifts, or the highest-profile opportunities, everyone else notices. And I can promise you they're keeping score. Even if favoritism isn't intentional, it feels personal to those left out. That's why fairness often requires you to check yourself.

I once worked with a manager who had a serious bias against an employee with a medical condition that caused frequent throat clearing. Now, was this employee bad at their job? No. Did their habit affect their work? Also no. But the sound annoyed the manager, and because of that, they snapped at this person more than anyone else. That's not fair. That's unintentional bias creeping in, creating unnecessary tension, and making the employee feel singled out over something beyond their control.

As a leader, it's your job to check your biases at the door and make sure your decisions are rooted in equity, not irritation. Fairness doesn't mean treating everyone exactly the same; it means ensuring everyone gets what they deserve based on trust, experience, and distribution of work.

When it comes to rewards like bonuses or raises, be transparent about how decisions are made. For instance, you could say, *"We're basing this year's raises on three factors: performance, tenure, and contributions to team goals. Here's how that breaks down."* This level of transparency builds trust and minimizes feelings of unfairness.

The thing about fairness is you'll know real fast if you're missing the mark because your team will tell you. Maybe not in the kindest, most professional way, but trust me, you'll hear about it. It might be through side-eye in meetings, passive-aggressive emails, or a sudden influx of "urgent" one-on-ones where people want to clarify something. If multiple people start hinting (or outright saying) that something feels unfair, it's worth a closer look.

Your team needs to trust that your decisions were made fairly. If they don't, get ready for the quiet mutiny of disengagement, because few things tanks morale faster than feeling like the game is rigged.

Keep the Tigers at Bay

At its core, the SCARF Model acknowledges that humans are wired for self-preservation. Our primary concern is staying alive. We are consistently scanning our environment for safety and hoping we don't get eaten by a metaphorical, or actual, predator. In the workplace, that predator isn't a saber-toothed tiger—it's uncertainty, lack of control, unfair treatment, or feeling undervalued. Our brains don't distinguish between actual danger and the gut-wrenching anxiety of a vague, "Hey, can we talk?"[8] Slack message from your boss. The response is the same: panic mode.

This is why people shut down, disengage, or get defensive when they feel threatened at work. If their status is questioned, if certainty is yanked away, if they don't have autonomy, if they feel disconnected from others, or if they sense unfairness, their brain switches from productive problem-solving to full-blown survival mode. And people in survival mode don't do their best work.

Your job as a leader is to keep the metaphorical tigers at bay. Understand that when people react emotionally, it's not because they're dramatic but because their brain is

---

[8] Do your team (and yourself) a favor and literally never say this to anyone. Be clear with an agenda item or two and a timeline for when you'd like to talk.

trying to protect them. When you recognize these triggers, you can lead with empathy, build a culture of trust, and make sure your team isn't wasting precious brainpower trying to decode whether their job (or sanity) is at risk.

By focusing on the SCARF Model, leaders can reduce the discomfort that triggers survival instincts and replace it with an environment where growth is inevitable. The next time you're faced with a leadership challenge, ask yourself:

- How can I recognize and elevate someone's **status**?
- What can I do to provide more **certainty** in this situation?
- Am I giving my team enough **autonomy** to make decisions and take ownership of their work?
- How can I foster **relatedness** and build trust within the team?
- Am I being **fair** and transparent in how I distribute work, rewards, and opportunities?

Give Grace to the Developing Brain

Let's talk about brains, specifically, those of our younger workforce. According to Joseph Ledoux's book, *The Emotional Brain*, the prefrontal cortex (part of the brain responsible for critical thinking, decision-making, and impulse control) doesn't fully develop in women until around age twenty-four and in men until around age twenty-six.[9]

That makes things really difficult for your twenty-two-year-old coworker. Sure, they're leading meetings, making decisions, and navigating responsibilities that feel huge. On paper, they're an adult. But neurologically, their brain is

---

[9] (Ledoux, 1998)

still wiring itself for long-term thinking, emotional regulation, and impulse control. It's like giving someone a fully stocked toolbox while they're still learning what each tool does and when to use it.

In the workplace, this explains why young adults, especially those in their early twenties, seem to operate with more emotion than logic. They're still growing into their ability to make fully reasoned, logical decisions. Society tends to expect eighteen-year-olds to be "adults" simply because they're legally of age. While they may *look* like adults, they're still running on a beta version of the adult brain with a few updates yet to install.

Emotions often take the wheel when the prefrontal cortex hasn't fully developed. For younger team members, this can mean big feelings—frustration, excitement, anxiety, joy—driving their responses to workplace situations. If you're managing a team of young twenty-somethings, you might notice that some of their reactions feel... dramatic. And honestly, they might be! But this isn't a reason to dismiss or criticize them. Instead, it's an opportunity to understand and meet them where they are.

While many of us grew up in homes that encouraged us to push those feelings down and "tough it out," that doesn't mean emotions go away. They're still there, bubbling under the surface, and they play a huge role in how we navigate the world. When these emotions bubble up in a member of your team, your role isn't to ignore or invalidate them. Your role is to guide them through the emotion with empathy and patience.

Some people operate with emotion in the driver's seat, while others lean more toward logic. Personally, I tend to camp out in the logic zone. I like to weigh decisions carefully and think things through. But even so, I still feel my feelings. Emotions are not the enemy of good decision-making. They're part of the process.

American culture and the patriarchy, however, tend to prioritize logic-based decisions over emotional ones. We value critical thinking, rational arguments, and data-driven choices. But this cultural preference can make us dismiss or downplay emotions as "irrational" or "unprofessional." That's a mistake. Emotions give us critical information about our needs, values, and motivations.

Often, young adults act in ways that remind us of toddlers by defaulting to black-and-white thinking or struggling with big feelings. We need to respond with the understanding that they are navigating emotions in a world that treats them like they're already "fully cooked." They're trying to make sense of adult expectations while their brains are still assembling the tools they need to thrive.

For example, they might struggle with:
- Managing emotional reactions in stressful situations.
- Feeling that to be successful, they have to say yes to everything.
- Understanding the long-term consequences of their decisions.
- Balancing their desire for independence with their need for guidance.
- Navigating work responsibilities and living an active (e.g. party) lifestyle.

This is where grace comes in. Instead of wondering why they don't "get it," we can approach them with empathy and a willingness to teach. Remember, these are opportunities to help them develop the skills and strategies they'll need for the rest of their lives.

When you take the time to meet younger employees where they are, you're setting them up for long-term growth. As they grow, they'll remember the leaders who took the time to understand and support them. They'll carry those lessons forward, becoming the empathetic, balanced leaders of tomorrow.

So, the next time you're working with a young team member and find yourself thinking, "Why don't they get it?" take a deep breath. Remind yourself that their brain is still growing, and they are doing the best they can with the tools they have. With your guidance, they'll learn to add more tools to their toolbox, and that's a win for everyone.

Leadership Will Be Messy

Leadership is not a static skill you master and check off your list. It's a constantly evolving adventure full of discomfort. Along the way, you'll experience a whirlwind of feelings: nervousness, fear, excitement, insecurity, surprise, and overwhelm—sometimes all at once. And that's normal.

Stress, especially when stepping into new roles, can be exhausting. You'll feel the fatigue creeping in, but there's also a good chance you will feel a surge of excitement as you tackle something new. That mix of emotions is a sign you're growing, and the best thing you can do is lean into it. Ride the wave. Embrace the discomfort.

In your first year as a manager, you probably won't feel like the best in the world at what you do. That's okay. It takes time to develop your authentic leadership style, to understand the cycles of managing employees, and to see what works for you. The truth is, even seasoned leaders— yes, including me as I write this—don't always feel 100% confident in their ability to manage. Every CEO I've worked with has had doubts. Every founder I know has faced intense fear before taking a big leap. The common thread? They felt the fear and did it anyway.

We are emotional beings. Those emotions aren't weaknesses. They exist to keep us alive, to guide us, and to teach us. Whether you grew up in a household that validated emotions or one that ignored them, I'm here to tell you: emotions are real, and understanding them is essential to being a great leader.

Chapter 3:
The Biology of Big Emotions

Your body doesn't make you feel things just for fun. Every emotion has a biological function designed to keep you alive. If you were wandering the wilderness three-thousand years ago and stumbled upon a bear, your body wouldn't wait for a polite introduction. Fear would hit, adrenaline would spike, and before you even fully processed what was happening, your legs would already be sprinting you toward safety.

Fast forward to today. There's a good chance you haven't run into a bear recently, but you have probably opened an email that sent your heart racing like you were about to be mauled. Maybe it was a vague "Hey, can we talk?" from your boss. Maybe it was a last-minute client request that made your stomach drop. The bear is gone, but your nervous system doesn't know that. Your body reacts the same way—tight chest, racing heart, heightened alertness—because in its opinion, danger is danger, whether it's a predator in the woods or a passive-aggressive Slack message. Understanding that emotions are designed to protect us means we can also start recognizing when they are overreacting to modern life. You don't need to outrun an email, but if your body is treating it like a life-threatening event, that's important information.

Unlike other bodily systems, like your cardiovascular system or your digestive system, emotions don't come with clear structures you can see on a scan. You can't take an X-ray of sadness or measure a pint of joy. Emotions are an intricate network of neurotransmitters, hormones, and physiological responses that influence how we navigate the world.

Lisa Feldman Barrett, a leading researcher in the field, has spent her career unpacking what emotions are and how they form in the body. In her book *How Emotions Are Made*, she says, "An emotion is your brain's creation of what your bodily sensations mean, in relation to what is going on around you in the world."[10] Meaning emotions aren't pre-programmed reactions that just "happen" to us. They are built from a combination of past experiences, social cues, and physiological responses. Your brain is actually *predicting* your emotions based on what's happening in your body.

This is why the same physical sensation can feel wildly different depending on context. A racing heart and sweaty palms could mean anxiety before a big presentation, but those same sensations could also mean excitement before getting on a rollercoaster. The body doesn't label emotions, but your brain does. Sometimes, it gets it wrong.

For example, I thought I had extreme pre-trip anxiety. I love traveling, but before every big trip, I'd be a ball of nerves. My chest would feel tight, my thoughts would race, and I'd convince myself I was feeling anxious. But then, in a conversation with a counselor, I learned that excitement and anxiety feel nearly identical in the body. The only difference is the story we attach to them. My body wasn't freaking out—it was excited for the trip.

Sometimes, emotions we don't fully recognize show up in strange ways. I remember a birthday when a friend

---

[10] (Barrett, 2018)

surprised me in the most thoughtful way. It was a completely positive experience, but I felt...angry? I had no reason to be mad, but there it was. A heat rising in my chest. It wasn't until I stopped to unpack it that I realized what was happening. I'd never been surprised like that before, and my brain wasn't sure how to categorize the overwhelming feeling. Beneath the anger, I was actually feeling surprise and love. But because I wasn't familiar with those two emotions flooding me at the same time, my brain defaulted to what it did recognize, which was anger.

The more we understand how emotions manifest in the body, the better we get at navigating them for the people we lead. Recognizing that an employee's frustration might be masking fear, or that someone's resistance to change could be rooted in uncertainty (or trauma, but we'll get to that later) rather than defiance, helps us lead with empathy instead of assumption.

Big Emotion Energy Comes for Us All

Have you ever been so deep in your feelings that logic packs its bags and heads for the hills? That's Big Emotion Energy—BEE for short—and trust me, it comes for all of us. No one is immune. Some people live in a permanent state of BEE, while others only get hit with a rogue emotional tsunami every so often. Either way, when BEE shows up, it's a full-body experience.

Humans generally fall into one of two camps when making decisions: logic-first or emotion-first. If you've ever taken a Myers-Briggs Type Index (MBTI) personality test, you've already seen this distinction. It's the third letter in your type. The "T" stands for Thinking, and the "F" stands for Feeling. In simple terms, thinkers prioritize logic, objectivity, and rational analysis, while feelers rely more on personal values and their own emotions

Despite how our professional world looks, 60% of the U.S. population identifies as feelers, while only 40% identify as thinkers.[11] Which is *shocking* to me. When it comes to management and leadership roles, thinkers are disproportionately promoted. The corporate world tends to favor the spreadsheet influenced "just the facts" approach, often skipping over feelers in favor of someone more "practical." But if the majority of our workforce makes decisions through the lens of emotion, why wouldn't we want that represented in leadership? Feelers don't only *feel*, they process situations deeply, lead with empathy, and make decisions that prioritize relationships.

Yet, no matter how you're wired, you should not make major decisions when you're in the middle of a BEE moment.

When you're angry, overwhelmed, stressed, or deep in any emotion, your brain isn't primed for decision-making. That's because your amygdala, the part of your brain responsible for processing emotions and responding to perceived threats, is running the show.[12] Think of it this way. When a toddler is having a meltdown, you don't sit them down and say, "Let's analyze this situation using logic." You comfort them. You offer a distraction. *You help them regulate.* Then, only after they are regulated can you have a conversation about what happened. Adults are no different.

---

[11] (Daniels, n.d.)
[12] (Guy-Evans, 2025)

When the Amygdala Takes the Wheel

There's a particular kind of moment that sneaks up on every leader, the kind that hijacks your nervous system before you even realize what's happening. One second, you're calm, composed, handling the day. The next, something sets you off. Maybe it's a sharp comment, an unexpected challenge, or a subtle power play. Your heart rate spikes. Your thoughts start racing. Your jaw tightens. Suddenly, your whole body is telling you to do something, anything, *right now.*

That's not clarity speaking. That's your amygdala. And it just hijacked your brain.

The term "amygdala hijack" refers to what happens when our brain's emotional center—the amygdala—decides that whatever's happening is threatening enough to sound the internal alarm.[13] In evolutionary terms, this is the part of your brain that used to save you from saber-toothed tigers. These days, it's more likely to react to a Slack message or a last-minute meeting request.

Once your brain believes you're in danger (emotional, psychological, or otherwise), it reroutes resources to protect the body. The part of your brain responsible for logic, reason, empathy, and patience goes offline. Your frontal lobe, which you might reasonably consider to be "you," isn't in charge anymore. Instead, your survival instincts take over.

This means your brain is not prioritizing collaboration, leadership, or problem-solving. It's focused on keeping you

---

[13] (Guy-Evans, Amygdala Hijack: How It Works, Signs, & How To Cope, 2023)

alive. Even though the "threat" might simply be a poorly worded email, your system doesn't know the difference. Which means you have become reactive, not reflective. You're not accessing your higher thinking. And you are absolutely not in the best state to make decisions that affect your team or your credibility.

When I feel that hijack happening, I've learned to recognize the pattern. For me, it's usually marked by a sudden, intense sense of urgency. If I let that feeling drive my behavior, I'll usually say or send something I'll regret because my headspace has been hijacked by fear, stress, or overwhelm. I'm not leading from my values at that moment. I'm leading from adrenaline.

This happens constantly in the workplace. A colleague contradicts us in a meeting, and we immediately imagine worst-case scenarios. Maybe we're being undermined, maybe we're going to get fired, maybe we're just not good enough. Our brains love to run that particular spiral. While it might feel empowering in the moment to fire off a scathing email or schedule a "clarifying" meeting, those actions are often driven by distorted stories we tell ourselves when we're frustrated. It feels like you're thinking, but you're reacting from a place of emotional unease.

This is where the anger iceberg comes into play.

The Anger Iceberg

Anger is one of the easiest emotions to see, but it's rarely the root emotion. Most of the time, anger is the tip of the iceberg, while the real feelings—fear, rejection, sadness, loneliness, frustration, and more—are lurking beneath the surface.

If a team member is angry (or if you are), pause and ask, what's really going on here?

Maybe they feel dismissed. Maybe they feel unappreciated. Maybe they're overwhelmed. If you don't take the time to explore what's underneath, all you're left with is raw, unchecked anger, and that doesn't lead to healthy communication.

This applies to self-awareness too. If you feel angry, but you don't take the time to sit with it, the emotion stays as anger. You have to let the emotion steep, just like tea. If you drop a tea bag in hot water and immediately pull it out, you don't get tea, you get slightly flavored water. Emotions work the same way.

Many people try to skip the steeping process and go straight to reacting. They fire off the email, make a sarcastic remark, or lash out before they understand why they're upset. But if you give yourself time to process, you might realize the issue runs deeper than you thought. Maybe the thing that made you angry today actually tapped into a long-standing issue that needs to be addressed. Or maybe, with a little time, you realize it wasn't worth addressing at all. Either way, before reacting, let the tea steep.

A great way to remind yourself of this? Print out an anger iceberg chart and put it somewhere you'll see it every day. Seriously. Google "anger iceberg" and find one that resonates with you. It's a simple but powerful visual that reinforces the idea that anger is usually a cover for something deeper. Here is the one I like to use:

WHAT WE SEE...

ANGER

WHAT'S BELOW THE SURFACE...

Sadness Guilt Fear
Shame Jealousy
Insecurity Loneliness
Scared Hurt Nervous
Embarassment

So, when your amygdala hijack starts, and what feels like anger courses through your veins, remind yourself it is likely a secondary emotion showing up to protect you from more vulnerable states like fear, embarrassment, shame, or another emotion that we might not even understand in the moment. If we lead from that masked emotion, we risk hurting the people we manage and the people we care about.

As managers, we need to know our own tells. If I notice I'm spiraling, and my chest is tight, and I'm narrating imaginary arguments in my head, that's when I know it's time to hit pause. Not reply. Not address it head-on. Take a pause. If my frontal lobe has checked out, it's not the time to take action. I don't want my amygdala sending emails on my behalf.

The same awareness applies to my team. If I notice a team member is visibly fried and they are snapping at colleagues, I try not to write it off as an attitude. More often than not, it's a hijack. Their nervous system has switched into survival mode, and they may not even realize it. In those moments, I don't scold. I send them home. I say, *"Hey, I can see you're running low today. Why don't you take the rest of the afternoon to reset? No emails, no meetings. Just rest. We'll pick it back up tomorrow."*

I wish I could shout this from the rooftops when I say that expecting any member of your team to push through when their amygdala is hijacked is poor leadership. When someone is in that activated state—heart racing, mind spinning, body locked in fight-or-flight—they're not able to think clearly, solve problems effectively, or engage with others in a healthy way. Their brain is literally prioritizing survival over logic, and pushing them to stay "productive" in that moment is counterproductive and unkind.

We've all had those days when something personal crashes into our professional space, or when a string of small stressors suddenly adds up to overwhelm. Forcing someone to keep going only increases the likelihood of mistakes, miscommunication, and emotional fallout. But when you give someone the space to reset (whether that's an afternoon off, a no-meeting day, or simply permission to step away and breathe) you're not losing productivity. You're investing in sustainability. They'll come back clearer, calmer, and far more capable of contributing in the way you hired them to.

I give myself the same grace. If I feel the hijack happening in me, I leave. I let someone else take point, I clear my calendar, and I make it clear to my team that I'm stepping away because I want to avoid saying or doing something I'll regret. That kind of self-awareness models exactly the kind of leadership I want my team to practice too.

Remember, the way you look leaving the room calmly is *always* better than the way you look snapping in front of your team. You can recover from stepping out. You can't always recover from what your hijacked brain says when it feels cornered. While you might think you're just venting or defending yourself, your brain is five years old and hopped up on cortisol. That is not the version of you your team deserves.

The better we get at recognizing the hijack and the emotions beneath the anger, the better we can choose when to speak, when to pause, and when to step back. Our goal isn't to eliminate strong emotion. That's not possible, and frankly, it's not desirable. Emotion is what makes us human. The goal is to know when it's driving and to gently guide it out of the front seat before it takes the whole car off a cliff.

How to Step out of the Storm

Once the amygdala has sounded the alarm, you can't just "calm down" through willpower. That ship has sailed. You're not going to logic your way out of a hijacked state because, your logic center isn't the one driving anymore.

That's why we need to get out of our heads—literally—and back into our bodies.

The fastest way I've found to shift emotional states is to move. A walk. A stretch. A literal shake-it-out moment like you're trying to fling bad vibes off your hands. Physical motion reminds your system that you are not under attack. You're safe. The simple act of walking, especially outdoors, begins to switch the brain back into a grounded, aware state.

Ideally, you're outside, off screens, out of artificial lighting, away from the Slack pings and kitchen sink judgment zone. If I need a quick reset, I'll head out the door and walk until I feel my feet again. Not metaphorically—*actually* feel my feet. The rhythm, the texture of the sidewalk, the resistance of shoes against the ground. That's my cue I'm coming back online.

If walking isn't an option or I need to stay put, I've got a backup plan. Door closed. Lights off. Phone silenced or turned off completely. No screens. No emails. No humans. Just me, low light, quiet, and a blanket if needed. I call this the cocoon phase. It's not glamorous, but it works. The goal is minimal sensory input to help your nervous system take a break.

Sometimes, though, what we really need is toddler love in the form of simple, grounding activities that regulate the nervous system with ease and immediacy. Think about what soothes a dysregulated toddler. It often involves movement, rhythm, sensory comfort, and connection. The same logic applies to adults.

So, what does toddler love look like in grown-up form?
- Coloring or doodling
- Going outside for fresh air and literally touching grass

- Taking deep, slow breaths
- Kicking a ball around or moving your body however feels good
- Listening to music that matches (or shifts) your emotional state

The goal isn't to ignore the emotion. It's to give it space so it doesn't take over. When we try to suppress it, power through, or pretend it's not happening, it doesn't go away. It gets louder.

This applies to your team, too. If you notice someone's off, maybe they are snapping in meetings, shutting down, or clearly overwhelmed, that's your cue to respond with grace, not pressure. Letting someone step away isn't coddling. It's human-centered leadership. It tells people that their well-being matters and that emotions are real. Sometimes, the most productive thing someone can do is pause.

If you really want to go the extra mile? Venmo them coffee money. Send them a treat via DoorDash. One of my favorite moves when someone on my team is having a bad day is surprising them with something small and kind. That act of generosity—especially in a moment of stress—can reinforce that you see them as a human being, not just a taskmaster.

What You're Feeling Is Valid—But That Story Might Be a Lie

Once you've walked it out, breathed it down, or cocooned yourself into a calmer nervous system, you're not quite done. You've turned the volume down in your head, but now it's time to deal with the *story* it left behind.

The trickiest thing about BEE is that even though the feeling is valid, the story you're telling yourself is often total fiction.

Let's say you're feeling furious. White-hot, unblinking, angry typing so loud everyone can hear. Your brain tells you, very convincingly, that the only path forward is to fire off that angry email. Or to have that confrontation. Or to say something that will finally make it clear how wrong the other person is. That's the story your brain has attached to the feeling because it's trying to find a resolution that matches the size of the sensation.

But that story isn't always accurate. In fact, when we're in big emotion energy, the story tends to be dramatic, absolute, and full of assumptions. It tells us if we don't act now, nothing will change. That we're being disrespected. That we're being excluded. That we're failing. That we're unsafe. The narrative spins fast, and it often doesn't leave room for nuance.

This is where we need to pause and interrogate the script. Start by questioning your assumptions:

- Is this story true?
- What evidence do I have to support that thought?
- What am I assuming here?

If the story is, "My boss is definitely trying to get rid of me," you can stop and ask, "Okay, what actual data do I have to support that?" Maybe the answer is a weird tone in an email. Maybe it's nothing. Maybe it's something. But the goal is to hold a light to the story and inspect it for holes.

For me, this is where the emotion wheel comes in handy. Especially if I'm feeling anger, and I know there is an underlying emotion beneath it, but I can't quite name that emotion. I'll take a closer look at the wheel and go through each feeling until one resonates. Usually, something clicks, and I realize, "Oh, I'm actually feeling embarrassed."

Once you've named the feeling under the feeling, practice self-validation.

Talk to yourself here like you'd talk to a good friend going through a difficult time. Say, "It makes sense that I'd feel this way." For me, if I'm scared of a change, I might say to myself, "Of course, I'm feeling scared right now. This is new and uncertain." Or, "It's normal that I'd feel disappointed when something I cared about didn't go the way I had hoped."

If it helps, think about that Pixar movies *Inside Out* or *Turning Red*. Emotions don't disappear because you're a grown-up. They just get sneakier, and they will get worse if you try to shove them down in a box and ignore them forever. You need to name the emotions, validate them, then inspect the story you're telling yourself.

So, if you're swirling, here's a quick list to follow. I recommend putting it on a sticky note in a place you can access quickly in times of emotional upset.

1. Name the feeling.
2. Check the story.
3. Validate the feeling without clinging to the fiction.
4. Give yourself grace.

Emotions are messengers, not mandates. They're there to tell us something, but not everything they say should be followed without question. You are still the leader of your inner team. Even when one of them shows up screaming in a red panda suit.

Before We Move On...

So far, we've explored what big emotions really are, including how they operate in the body, how they hijack our thinking, and how to come back to center when the storm hits. But recognizing them is only the first step.

Sooner or later, you're going to find yourself leading in the middle of a big emotion. You'll be the one triggered, overwhelmed, or stretched thin, and in that moment, people will still be looking at you. That's why the next chapter isn't just about surviving your own emotions. It's about leading *through* them, without letting them lead *you*.

Chapter 4:
Leading with Big Feelings of Your Own

In times of uncertainty or rapid change, it's perfectly normal for our emotions to spike beyond the usual. Most days, we operate from baseline. We handle the meetings, the emails, the interruptions. But when our baseline gets shaken and the ground underneath us starts to shift, our feelings come rushing in like a wave. And sometimes, those feelings are the ones leading the meeting instead of us.

I remember one of those moments vividly. We were in the thick of it. Our organization had gone through its *second* CEO change in less than a year. Leadership was churning like a washing machine, and word on the street was that a reorg was coming…*again*. The tension was high, and honestly? We were exhausted.

One morning, our team was called into the COO's office without our supervisor. The request came out of the blue with no context. Just a calendar ping and a knot in the stomach. As we stepped into the elevator, one of my direct reports, who was also a close friend and colleague, turned to me and quietly asked, "Is it okay if I ask questions?"

And I, without skipping a beat or offering any reason or reassurance, said, "No." The word acted like a one-word wall between me and her. The look she gave me in response could have melted steel as she processed her hurt, confusion, and disbelief. It was the kind of look that silently says, Who are you right now?

The truth is, I didn't fully realize what I had done until later. At that moment, I was scared. We didn't know what we were walking into when we got called into that meeting, and my instinct was to protect. To shield the people I cared about by clamping down on anything that might make it so I couldn't control the situation. But in doing that, I shut someone down who didn't deserve it. I let fear drive the interaction, and fear is a terrible chauffeur. It rarely takes you anywhere you actually want to go.

We walked into the meeting and learned we'd be reporting to a new VP. It was exactly the kind of change we'd been bracing for, but that didn't make it any easier. Still, we got through it. Afterward, as we debriefed and started to make sense of what came next, I finally took a breath and owned it.

"I'm sorry," I told her. "I was scared. I felt protective. But I trust you. That answer shouldn't have been no. I was wrong."

With those words, we were able to move past the moment because I acknowledged it. Simply naming what's true, without fixing or defending, can lower the temperature in a room. This can happen to any one of us, especially when change is on the horizon and we aren't sure of our future. When our big emotions show up unannounced, they can speak on our behalf in ways that don't reflect who we really are.

At that moment, I lost some of the trust I had built up with this team member. When that happens, the best thing you can do is repair it, quickly. If you said something that didn't land well or came off unkind, own it as soon as you realize it. Don't wait days. Rip off the band-aid and say the words. A verbal apology is always best when possible, but depending on the situation, a quick text can be better than waiting too long to make it right.

We need to be able to recognize when our fear or stress is doing the talking. We need to be willing to name it, to apologize, to recalibrate if our emotions get the better of us. Because at times, they will get the better of us. Our teams don't expect us to be perfect. But they do need us to be real. And in the messy, high-pressure moments—especially the ones we don't handle well—the most powerful thing we can offer is honesty.

We Have All These Feelings... Now What?

Okay, so we've established that emotions are real, unavoidable, and sometimes hit us like an unexpected tidal wave. But what do we *do* with all of that? How do we navigate our own emotions and the emotions of others, especially when we're in leadership roles and people are looking to us for stability?

Let's take a closer look at Daniel Goleman and the research that led to the books *Primal Leadership*[14] and *Resonant Leadership*[15] (both great reads I'd recommend). Goleman took the dense, brainy science of emotions and translated it into something the rest of us can actually use. No neuroscience degree required. He's written multiple

---

[14] (Goleman, 2013)
[15] (Boyatzis & McKee, 2005)

books on the topic, and if you ever want to impress someone at a leadership conference, casually drop his name and nod like you've been quoting him for years.

Goleman breaks emotional intelligence down into four key pillars, all of which are critical for effective leadership:

1. **Self-Awareness**: Understanding your own emotions, triggers, and patterns.
2. **Self-Management**: Regulating those emotions so they don't hijack your decision-making.
3. **Awareness of Others**: Recognizing and interpreting the emotions of those around you.
4. **Relationship Management**: Using that awareness to build strong, effective relationships.

These Four Pillars of Emotional Intelligence are the sturdy foundation that keeps everything else from collapsing into chaos. Mastering these means you can navigate your emotions with purpose, instead of stuffing them inside a box. Now, let's break these pillars down one by one.

Self-Awareness: The Art of Not Being an Accidental Asshole

Before you can manage your emotions, you need to know what they are. Sounds simple, right? Except that most of us are walking around with a swirling cocktail of feelings, completely unaware of what's happening inside our own heads and bodies.

Practicing self-awareness means pressing pause and checking in with yourself both mentally and physically.

What's showing up in your body? Is your chest tight? Are your hands clammy? Do you suddenly have the overwhelming urge to yell at someone for breathing too loudly? (Pro tip: That last one might be a sign you're stressed.)

The key is to identify what you're feeling before it spills out in unhelpful ways. Anxiety, fear, boredom, frustration, whatever it is, you need to name it. If you don't, you're going to start making decisions based on emotions you haven't even acknowledged, and that's how people end up sending regrettable emails or snapping at their barista.

Let's say it's Monday night, and you get devastating news—a friend has passed away. Right now, you don't quite believe what has happened, but come tomorrow, grief will be setting in. The self-aware move is to take the time to recognize that grief will impact your emotional state and make choices accordingly. Typically, that might mean calling out of work or letting your team know you're not at full capacity.

The alternative, of course, is not acknowledging it (which many of us unfortunately do) and pushing through it. Likely becoming a complete nightmare to be around as your emotions make it difficult to think clearly. Unprocessed emotions don't go away. They leak. If you don't recognize you are grieving, you might find yourself being short with people, reading way too much into someone's Slack message, or feeling inexplicably furious that your coworker dared to ask how your weekend was. It's not really about them. It's about what's going on inside of you.

Self-awareness requires pausing, tuning in, and actually sitting with what you're feeling instead of stuffing it down and hoping for the best. Let's be honest—most of us were not taught how to do this growing up. School didn't exactly offer a "How to Identify and Regulate Your Feelings 101" class, and unless you had emotionally intelligent parents (lucky you), you probably picked up emotional habits from watching the adults around you. Which might not have been the healthiest crash course.[16]

But the good news is that it's never too late to start. A great tool I like to use is the Emotion Wheel. Google it and you'll find several examples. This handy chart maps out core emotions and their subcategories, helping you pinpoint

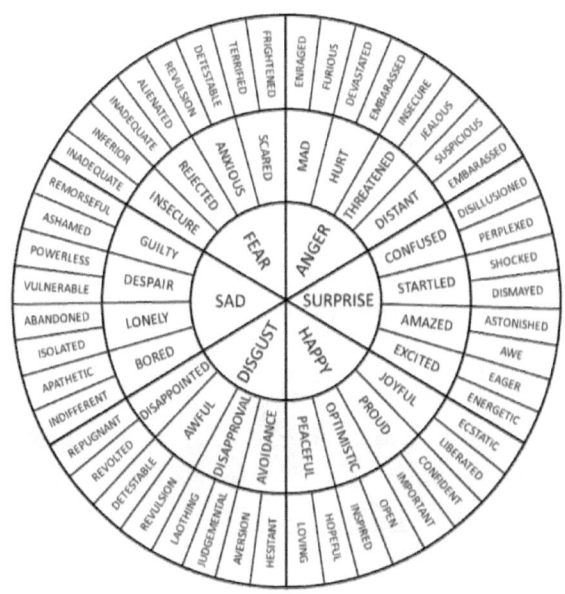

---

[16] While feeling our emotions is important, sometimes it's okay to put our feelings on the shelf until we can get somewhere safe. Let's say you hear the news about your friend's passing while you're at the office. It's okay not to feel your feelings in that moment. Wrap up what you need to, then head to a place where you can safely feel your feelings.

what you're feeling. "I'm mad" might actually mean "I'm disappointed," and "I'm anxious" might really be "I'm overstimulated."

If you want a basic guide to core emotions, think of the movie *Inside Out*. Seriously. That movie certainly wasn't only for kids; it was an emotional intelligence masterclass. The main characters Joy, Anger, Sadness, Fear, and Disgust represent our core emotions, and they develop in stages:

- As toddlers, we get hit with the first wave: joy, anger, and sadness. Because we have zero coping skills, they show up big. This is why a toddler drops their cookie and reacts like it's the end of the world, because in their emotional experience, it is.
- Then puberty hits, and suddenly, we unlock new, complex emotions. Except nobody explains what they are, why they feel so intense, or how to handle them. So, we're left trying to figure it out while also dealing with acne, high school drama, and questionable fashion choices.

From there, the journey of emotional intelligence is entirely up to you. If you grew up in a household where emotions were validated, you probably started this work early. If you didn't (raises hand), you might be starting now. This book might be your point one, the moment you start intentionally learning what emotions are, where they show up in your body, and how to navigate them. Welcome to the party!

The more you understand your own emotions, the healthier your relationships will be, the stronger your leadership will become, and the more authentically you can show up in your life. So, if you take nothing else from this chapter, take this: Pause. Identify what you're feeling. And don't let unprocessed emotions turn you into an accidental asshole.

Self-Management: Getting a Grip Before You Flip

So, you've identified what you're feeling but now comes the challenge of managing those feelings. Self-awareness without self-management is like realizing your house is on fire and deciding to stand there and watch rather than do something.

Self-management is about regulating emotions in a way that keeps you from making impulsive decisions, saying things you'll regret, or spiraling into emotional chaos. It's not about suppressing feelings. It's about knowing how to navigate them before they navigate you.

When our emotions spike, our heart rate follows. Once our heart rate climbs past ninety beats per minute, our brain essentially flips the emergency switch. This is called flooding.

Flooding happens when your brain gets hit with a tidal wave of stress hormones—like adrenaline and cortisol—all at once. Then your prefrontal cortex, the part of your brain responsible for logic, decision-making, and impulse control, essentially short-circuits. Studies have shown that under extreme emotional stress, neurons in the prefrontal cortex disconnect and stop firing properly, meaning rational thinking *literally* goes offline.[17]

This is why, in the middle of an argument or a high-stress situation, you might be unable to think clearly, say

---

[17] (Arnsten, Mazure, & Sinha, 2012)

things you regret, or feel completely overwhelmed. Your brain is prioritizing survival over logic, treating the situation like an immediate threat, even if that "threat" is a tense email or a difficult conversation.

When flooding happens, the best thing to do is pause, breathe, and step away. Trying to solve a problem while your brain is in full meltdown mode is like trying to fix a car while it's still speeding down the highway.

Which means?
- Now is not the time to send that email.
- Now is not the time to give performance feedback.
- Now is not the time to confront your coworker about stealing your yogurt from the office fridge.

When you're emotionally flooded, problem-solving is off the table. Instead, you need to focus on getting your nervous system back to baseline before engaging with anything important.

Tactics for Bringing Yourself Back Down
1. Breathe Like You Mean It

Breathwork is the MVP of emotional regulation. Your breathing and nervous system are besties, and when you control one, you can influence the other. Intentional breathing sends a signal to your brain that you're safe, which helps bring your heart rate down and gets your prefrontal cortex (aka logic brain) back online.

It could be as simple as forcing yourself to take three slow, deep, breaths. Or you could utilize a strategy called square breathing, where you inhale for four counts, hold for four, exhale for four, hold for four. Repeat. (Think of it like drawing a mental square—simple, structured, effective.)

The trick is you must do it consciously. Your body won't magically reset without your help, so take those deep breaths like you mean it.

2. Walk It Off (Literally)

When I'm feeling "zingy," meaning my emotions are running high and my body is practically vibrating, I walk.

When you walk, your brain kicks into gear, releasing endorphins, serotonin, and norepinephrine, all of which boost your mood and lower stress.[18] At the same time, increased blood flow and oxygen to the brain enhance memory, focus, and problem-solving skills, which explains why some of the best ideas happen mid-stride.[19] If you're outside, the benefits double. Nature exposure has been shown to lower activity in brain regions linked to depression, while sunlight helps regulate your circadian rhythm, improving sleep and overall mental health.[20] Let's not forget the simple magic of distraction, walking provides fresh stimuli that help interrupt negative thought loops, giving your brain a much-needed reset.

So next time you're feeling stuck, overwhelmed, or a little zingy, try taking a walk. Science says it works, and honestly, so do I. Go slow or fast, it doesn't matter, just move. If you are still feeling zingy when you get back, take another lap.

------

[18] (Does walking for mental health actually improve wellbeing?, n.d.)

[19] (Rogers, 2022)

[20] (Jordan, 2015)

Personally, I don't try to work when I feel these big emotions because it often leads to sloppy mistakes. If I'm emotionally flooded, my decision-making is compromised, and that's when typos, bad calls, and regrettable replies happen. Better to reset first, then tackle the task.

3. Sunlight Is Nature's Free Therapy

We are solar-powered beings. Some of us need more sunlight than others, but I am personally convinced that my body runs on sunshine. Even on cold days, stepping outside for a few minutes grounds me and resets my mood. There's something about feeling the warmth on your skin, even if the air is crisp, that reminds your nervous system everything is fine.

Science backs this up. Sunlight boosts vitamin D,[21] which plays a huge role in mood regulation, brain function, and even immune health. Low vitamin D levels have been linked to increased anxiety and depression,[22] which means that a little sunshine is a biological necessity. Sunlight also helps regulate your circadian rhythm,[23] which affects sleep quality, and let's be real, everything in life feels harder when you're exhausted.

Beyond the chemical benefits, sunlight is a state-changer. It shifts your perspective. Have you ever been in a terrible mood, gone outside, and suddenly felt a little bit better? That's because exposure to natural light lowers

---

[21] (Akpınar & Karadağ, 2022)
[22] (Akpınar & Karadağ, 2022)
[23] (Ridenour, 2024)

activity in the parts of the brain associated with stress and overthinking.[24]

And let's not forget that it's really hard to stay angry when you're standing in warm, golden light on a nice day. Science for the win.

4. Water Is an Emotional Reset Button

If you're more of a water person, try showering, swimming, or even just splashing cold water on your face. There's a reason people say, "Take a cold shower and cool off." Water literally changes your physiological state.[25]

When you expose your body to water, especially cool or cold water, your nervous system responds immediately. Cold water triggers the dive reflex, which slows your heart rate, reduces stress hormones, and activates the parasympathetic nervous system, the part of your body responsible for calming you down.[26] This is why plunging your face into cold water can stop a panic attack in its tracks.

Beyond the cold-water shock effect, any form of water immersion can help regulate emotions. Swimming, floating, or even standing under the shower creates a full-body sensory experience that signals to your brain that it's time to reset. The rhythmic motion of swimming, the sound of water rushing past your ears, or the simple ritual of

---

[24] (Kent, 2023)

[25] For the astrology fans here, I'm a fire sign, so this doesn't work for me. But if you're a water sign, a Pisces in distress, or just someone who finds peace in a bath, this one's for you.

[26] (Using the Diver's Reflex to Regulate Emotional Intensity, 2022)

washing away the day can all bring a sense of physical and emotional relief.

I like to do a cold plunge every Sunday. While the routine is still fairly new, I'm already hooked. Don't get me wrong, it is as *awful* as it sounds, but I get through it by believing I am tougher than cold water. The worst part comes in the first ten seconds. Your body feels intense shock, and this is where I usually make some loud, awkward, squally noises. I'm waiting for the day a neighbor hears and peaks their head over the fence to see what the heck I'm up to.

After the initial "wowza" sensation, my body goes to work protecting its essentials. My vessels constrict, and resources get sent to the cells that need them most. I can almost feel old injuries healing while I'm immersed. It's also deeply rewarding to see my times improve. My first plunge was about two minutes, while my most recent plunge was up to sixteen minutes (don't worry, I don't plan to cold plunge for much longer than that). The cold water helps my body heal what it needs to, and the exercise gives me a *major* sense of accomplishment. It is a weekly reminder that I can do hard things. Ten seconds of being incredibly uncomfortable has a payoff that's worth it for me.

5. Do a Body Scan to Check Yourself Before You Wreck Yourself

If you ever find yourself randomly furious or anxious for no reason, it could be because your body is holding onto tension you didn't even realize was there. A body scan is a quick mental check-in with every part of yourself.

Start at your feet and work your way up:

- Wiggle your toes. Move your ankles.
- Check in with your legs, hips, and torso.
- When you hit the neck, jaw, and shoulders—pause and take your time. That's where most people store stress.

Guided body scans are everywhere (YouTube, meditation apps, etc.), but once you get the hang of it, you can do a mini check in under a minute. If you're constantly clenching your shoulders, grinding your teeth, or feeling tight in your chest, that's your body's way of telling you something needs to change.

Finally, I want you to remember that self-care is not a luxury, it's maintenance. You don't wait to change the oil once it's all leaked out (and if you do, your car's already in trouble). The same goes for your body and your brain. If you only reach for self-care when you're spiraling, it's already too late. The goal is to build a consistent practice that keeps your mental wellness tank full before it hits empty. When you're running on fumes, your emotions take the wheel, and they're terrible drivers.

So, let's make a plan:

- When you feel flooded, take a breath before you react.
- When you feel zingy, walk it off.
- When you feel stuck, check in with your body.

I'll try to do the same.

Awareness of Others: Pay Attention or Pay the Price

Noticing people (really noticing them) is part observation, part communication, and a whole lot of presence. And let's be honest, presence isn't exactly our default setting. Most of us are about as observant as a raccoon in a room full of shiny objects.

Unless we make a conscious effort to notice the people around us, we're going to miss things. When you're in a leadership role, missing things doesn't only mean forgetting who took the last donut in the break room; it also means missing opportunities to support your team when they need it most.

Think about your team. You probably already know their general habits, even if you've never really thought about it. How do they sit in meetings? Do they lean in when they're engaged, or do they slouch back? What do they usually wear? Are they button-down people, hoodie people, or somewhere in between? What's their normal level of participation in conversations?

Some people are naturally more animated, while others are more reserved. Some people keep their cameras off in virtual meetings as a rule, while others always turn them on. These habits are all part of their baseline, and when you pay attention to them over time, you start to recognize what is typical for each person.

That baseline is what allows you to recognize when something is off. If your usually talkative employee is suddenly quiet and withdrawn, that's worth noticing. If the person who always shows up in a crisp button-down suddenly comes in wearing the same wrinkled t-shirt three days in a row, that's a clue. If someone who typically jumps in with ideas during brainstorming sessions is unusually checked out, that tells you something.

These shifts in behavior don't automatically mean there's a crisis, but they do mean something has changed. As a leader, noticing those changes and checking in is part of the job.

This same concept applies to communication patterns. Most people have a preferred way of reaching out: maybe they're an email person, a Slack DM person, or a classic texter. If someone who always emails you suddenly starts sending direct messages, or if they typically text when they're running late but now, they've called instead, that deviation from their normal behavior is worth paying attention to.

Step one is to establish baseline behaviors and communication patterns for the people you work with. Pay attention to what is normal for each person, because when something shifts outside of that normal range, it can be a signal that they need support. Maybe nothing is wrong, but maybe something is. The only way to know is to check in.

Step two is to take a breath, ground yourself, and approach the situation with curiosity instead of assumption. If someone is acting differently, resist the urge to immediately make it about you or about work. It's easy to jump to conclusions and think, are they mad at me? Did I do something wrong? But most of the time, people's emotional states have nothing to do with you.

A simple, non-intrusive check-in can go a long way. Something like, *"Hey, I noticed you're a little quieter than usual today. Everything okay?"* This gives them space to share if they want to, without forcing them to explain if they're not ready. When you make a habit of noticing others, you can show up for people in ways that matter and ask the right questions at the right time.

Relationship Management: Keep Calm and Lead On

Relationship management is about how we communicate, when we communicate, and how much patience we bring to the table while doing it.

One of the biggest traps we fall into when managing relationships is urgency. When we feel big emotions, it feels like we need to solve the issue right away. But unless you're literally saving babies (which, I'm guessing, you're not), then nothing is so urgent that it can't wait for you to process your emotions first. This is where patience comes in. Pick a tactic for bringing yourself back down, and make sure you are calm before addressing anyone else.

In these moments, it helps me to remember that everyone is doing the best they can with the tools they have. Even the annoying people (the ones who cut you off in traffic or leave aggressive comments in email threads) have some kind of logic driving their choices. It might not be *your* logic, but it's theirs. So, how do we navigate that?

We need to be aware of what we're feeling and communicate it. Lean into vulnerability and name your emotions. Then, help your team do the same. A lot of people aren't great at identifying their own emotions in the moment, so as a leader, it's helpful to give them a starting point.

For example, if someone seems tense or withdrawn, you could say, *"It seems like you might be feeling frustrated. Is that right?"* If they agree, great, you're helping them put words to what they're feeling. If not, they'll correct you, which still opens the door for better communication. Either way, the goal is to help make emotions part of the conversation, not something to be avoided.

A great way to structure this is through "I feel" statements, a method developed by the Gottman Institute (they've built an entire research empire on understanding relationships).[27] This method is a simple yet wildly effective way to communicate emotions without turning conversations into blame games.

It follows a three-part formula:

I feel [emotion] *when* [specific situation], *and I need* [request for resolution].

So, instead of saying, "You never listen to me," you'd say, *"In that meeting last week, I felt unheard and disrespected. I was interrupted multiple times and wasn't able to complete my thoughts. In these meetings, I want to feel safe and respected."*

This approach works because it communicates emotions clearly without assigning blame. Instead of saying, "You disrespected me," which immediately makes people defensive, you're explaining how you felt and why. That small shift makes all the difference in relationship management.

Another essential skill is the pause. If you're emotionally flooded, you cannot keep your mouth shut, and you're about to say something you'll regret, you need a break. There is nothing wrong with stepping away before having a difficult conversation. A simple, *"I need a couple*

---

[27] (Benson, 2017)

of days to process this. Let's talk later this week about how we want to move forward," can save you from unnecessary conflict and allow for better, more thoughtful communication.

If someone communicates something in a way that is hurtful or feels targeted, remember, their communication is likely not about you. People will be amazing, and people will also be absolute jerks. Neither of those things have anything to do with you. They are operating based on their own experiences, their own challenges, and their own realities. That doesn't mean you shouldn't address problems, but it does mean you shouldn't take everything personally.

There's an old rule that says if something still bothers you after twenty-four hours, bring it up within forty-eight hours. That's a solid rule to follow. When emotions run high, it can feel like you need to address it *right now*. But if you wait twenty-four hours, you'll usually have a better perspective on the situation.

Use that time to process. Ask yourself:

- Did this person really intend to make me feel this way?
- Is this a one-time mistake or a pattern?
- What's the best way to approach this conversation constructively?

Understanding emotional intelligence gives us the tools to name, manage, and navigate our feelings with intention. But even with all that awareness, there are days when you simply don't have the capacity to lead with your full self. Maybe you're running on little sleep, juggling personal stress, or just feeling emotionally spent. That's where the Spoon Theory comes in.

The Spoon Theory

Why did I snap like that in the elevator? Why did "no" come out of my mouth like a reflex instead of the reassuring words my team needed? Because I was out of spoons.

Let's talk about the Spoon Theory, which originally came from Christine Miserandino, who used it to explain what it's like to live with a chronic illness like lupus. She handed her friend twelve actual spoons and said, "Okay, every single thing I do today, including getting dressed, making breakfast, taking the bus, showing up for work, costs me one of these. Once I'm out, I'm out."[28] Each spoon represents a unit of energy (mental, physical, or emotional). And for some people, especially those dealing with illness or burnout, that energy is limited and must be carefully rationed.

It was meant to help folks understand what energy management looks like for people living with chronic illness. But over time, it found its way into other spaces, especially special education and mental health circles, and for good reason. In reality, we're all walking around with a limited number of spoons, and we don't all start with the same number each day.

Let's say you typically start the day with twelve spoons. Maybe you woke up late. Spoon gone. Maybe your kid was in rare form over breakfast. Spoon gone. Maybe traffic was a mess, you spilled your coffee in your lap, and

---

[28] (Miserandino, 2003)

you forgot your laptop charger. That's three spoons gone, easy. Now it's nine-fifteen am and you've got seven spoons left to get through a whole workday. *Good luck.*

We've all felt those moments, where the day just started and yet we already feel exhausted. The moment I snapped "no" in the elevator, I was emotionally bankrupt. Sleep-deprived. Leadership-weary. Hadn't eaten a nutrient-dense meal in days. Whatever resilience I normally show up with was tapped. My "best self" didn't stand a chance because I had no spoons left to give.

When we're out of spoons, we don't lead, we react. That's why spoon management matters so much, especially when you're responsible for other people. Showing up to lead a team with zero spoons is like showing up to host a dinner party with no food in the fridge. You might be able to fake it for a few minutes, but eventually everyone's going to notice, and someone's going to be disappointed.

This is why I now try to be upfront with my team. I'll literally say, *"Hey, just a heads up, I'm running low on spoons today. I've got maybe five spoons on me, and three of those are already spoken for. So, if it's not urgent, let's push it to tomorrow."* This comment helps set expectations and budget my emotional energy.

As a manager, your brain is constantly scanning for potential conflict, morale shifts, and undercurrents no one's saying out loud. You're fielding questions, absorbing reactions, moderating tone, and calibrating your own responses in real time. You're expected to model calm, fairness, and thoughtfulness even when you're personally under pressure. It's not only the work you do that's exhausting, but also the emotional labor of being the buffer between the team and the chaos. That ongoing demand on your nervous system adds up, and unless you're actively keeping an eye on it, it's only a matter of time before you have no spoons left to give.

When you are up front about your energy capacity, you signal to your team that they should be as well. Whether you realize it or not, your team is constantly looking to you for cues. They're wondering: Is it safe to take a breath? Is it okay to say, "I need a minute"? If you normalize boundaries, rest, and honest conversations about capacity, they'll start to believe they can too. You're modeling what sustainable leadership looks like. That means when they hit their wall, they won't push through out of fear; they'll pause, recalibrate, and return stronger.

Know Thy Spoon Triggers

Now let me be clear, not all spoons are spent equally. There are some tasks I can do on autopilot—like answering emails, scheduling a meeting, or checking in with a teammate. Those cost me maybe a quarter of a spoon. But other things? Full spoon. Sometimes two.

Like the grocery store. If I only need milk and bananas, I'm fine. But a full shop? With a list? And crowds? And seventeen brands of marinara sauce all daring me to pick wrong? That's a multi-spoon event. There are just too many decisions, too many carts in too many aisles, and way too many people. This is why I pivoted to Instacart. Now, my grocery shopping doesn't burn any spoons. It's a no-timelines-imposed solution I can do while in my pajamas. I deeply enjoy it and find it worth the money. It's a gift to my nervous system and a public service to the people who would've had to witness me muttering in the sauce aisle.

The same goes for commuting. For some folks, the drive to work is meditative. For me, it's a spoon siphon. Don't even get me started on mass transit. I recently took a trip that involved trains, subways, walking, maps, and conversations like, "Wait, which line are we on?" By the end of it, I was cooked. Not tired, *cooked*. Done. No decisions left in me. No social battery to spare. I needed food, a nap, and a no-talking zone immediately. Of course, that was the same day I accidentally locked myself out of the Airbnb. Classic, right? I sat right down on the sidewalk, let the wall hold me up, and handed the logistics baton to my partner, who still had a few spoons left to get us through.

When you're out of spoons, you're *out*. There is no "dig deep and power through." There is only "sit down, regroup, and maybe cry a little if you need to." Sometimes the spoon dump is slow and happens throughout a stressful morning, a surprise deadline, and a string of back-to-back meetings. Other times it's sudden. Like a phone call with bad news. Or your kid throwing up in the backseat. Or, I don't know, a police officer sideswiping your car.

That last one actually happened. It was 8:15 am, I was almost at the office, and—bam!—my mirror's dangling and I'm blinking at a police SUV that had just grazed my precious Honda Fit. Now, on another day, that might have unhinged me. I might have stormed out of the car, started a full-blown rant, maybe even cried or called someone to vent.

But that day? I had spoons. I was rested, it was morning, and nothing else spoon draining had happened yet. So instead of spiraling, I walked into a nearby coffee shop while the rookie cop called his supervisor, grabbed a latte, and thought, "Well... this is definitely going to be a story." And it was fine. A little absurd, sure, but fine. The kind of fine that only happens when you've got the emotional reserves to roll with it. But if that same thing had happened at 5:30 pm, after a long day of meetings, conflict, and burnt coffee? That rookie might've met a very different version of me. One that didn't have any coffee-buying grace to offer.

We like to think we're consistent people. But we're not—we're contextual. And the context of our emotional energy matters more than we give it credit for.

Leading by Example
(Even When You're Low on Spoons)

Emotions aren't a glitch in the system. They're part of the operating manual that makes us human. Yet, many leaders try to push them down, ignore them, or box them up so their team never sees them.

As human beings, we're going to have days when those emotions are bigger than usual. Days when the unexpected knocks the wind out of us. Days when our drawer is empty before we even sit down at our desk. That's not a weakness. That's being alive. Allow your team to see those moments.

The work of real, grounded, human-centered leadership isn't about having it together all the time. It's about recognizing when you don't. It's about noticing when big emotion energy has taken over and choosing not to power through at the expense of yourself or your team.

You don't have to stand at the front of the room and say, "Class is now in session on emotional regulation." You have to show up differently. Consistently. Honestly. When your spoons are gone, you step out instead of snapping. When your brain is hijacked, you take a walk instead of writing a manifesto. When you feel big feelings, you name them, move through them, and come back when you're calm again.

Your team will watch you choose calm over urgency. Integrity over reactivity. Care over control. Slowly, they'll learn to do the same without you ever having to tell them to. That's how real change happens in the workplace through modeling, not telling.

When you choose to step away rather than snap, when you prioritize self-awareness over performance, when you pause instead of reacting, you're sending a message to everyone around you. You're saying that it's okay to say, "I'm not at my best today." That it's okay to take a breath before responding. That it's okay to make room for the full emotional experience of being a person in a workplace.

When leadership makes space for that, everyone else can too. But that kind of openness doesn't happen by default. Most employees have been conditioned, sometimes for years, to believe that showing emotion at work is risky. That saying "I'm not okay today" might be interpreted as weakness, instability, or worse—*a liability*. After all, when your paycheck, your healthcare, and your entire livelihood are tied to your perceived performance, it can feel downright dangerous to let your guard down. Even the most compassionate workplace won't override that instinct unless leaders go first.

That's why the ripple effect of your choices matters so much. When you normalize honest conversations about capacity, when you say out loud that you're stepping away to regroup, when you check in on someone instead of pushing them harder, you're creating a new blueprint. One that doesn't require people to white-knuckle their way through bad days.

Chapter 5:

Why We Do Anything at All

Humans are not nearly as complex as we like to think we are. At least not when it comes to why we do stuff. If you've ever given a toddler a Skittle for peeing in the potty or slipped your dog a treat for sitting on command, congratulations, you've dabbled in behaviorism. You, like millions before you, have tapped into the basic levers of human (and canine) motivation, reward, and punishment.

This isn't a new idea. Behaviorism has been around for ages, thanks to people like B.F. Skinner and John Watson, who believed that all human action could be explained by external consequences. Want someone to do something? Reward them. Want them to stop doing something? Punish them. Rinse, repeat, and hope you don't end up creating a monster.

In the workplace, behaviorism shows up in things like performance bonuses, employee-of-the-month plaques, pizza parties, and the dreaded performance improvement plan (PIP). It's the old carrot-and-stick approach, and if you've ever held a job, you've likely experienced both ends of that deal.

Now, to be clear, punishment isn't where I recommend starting. You don't create psychological safety by threatening timeouts. But let's not pretend it doesn't happen. A difficult one on one, a demotion, being excluded from important meetings—those are just workplace-friendly versions of a slap on the wrist. Or in toddler terms, no screen time.

For parents, behaviorism often becomes a go-to tool. If you've ever said, "If you put your shoes on, you can have a fruit snack," you've tapped into the behavioral playbook. It is a kind of shared language we use to create cooperation, especially when life is hectic. And sometimes, in the beautiful chaos of parenting, a little fruit snack leverage goes a long way.

So, why are we talking about this in a book on human-centered management?

Because this framework—basic as it is—sets us up to understand the next big leap in motivation theory. It helps explain why we do anything at all. If behaviorism says we move toward the cookie or away from the consequence, then motivation theory asks a more nuanced question: What if we're doing it because we care? What if someone shows up not for the gold star or the threat of a stern email, but because they genuinely want to?

That's the world of intrinsic motivation, and it's the real magic. It's the steady drive fueled by curiosity, purpose, and the satisfaction of doing something because it matters to you. When you understand that, you start managing people differently. You stop asking, "How do I get them to do this?" and start asking, "Why would they want to?" That is a very different kind of leadership.

Intrinsic vs. Extrinsic Motivation

Let's break down the two major categories of motivation. Think of extrinsic motivation as the junk food of human behavior. It's easy, it's convenient, and it gives you a short-term boost, but it's not exactly nourishing. It's the deal you make when you tell yourself, "I'll do this thing because I'll get something in return." That thing might be a paycheck, a bonus, a gold star, or free pizza for helping a friend move, but it is always something you are receiving outside of yourself.

Extrinsic motivation is transactional by design. It's everywhere, and it's not all bad. Our entire traditional education system runs on it. Grades, prizes, and honor rolls are all part of extrinsic motivation we use to push students. Most workplaces use it too. Perform well, and you might get a bonus. Miss the mark, and you might get a PIP.

But research shows that relying solely on extrinsic motivators may actually reduce our enjoyment, creativity, and engagement. In one experiment, college students were asked to complete puzzles. Some were paid for each one they completed, while others were not. After a 30-minute session, the researchers left the room for exactly eight minutes to see if the students would keep puzzling or do something different.

The students who had been paid stopped puzzling as soon as the researcher left. The students who weren't paid kept going. They kept puzzling because they were genuinely enjoying it. In other words, payment diluted internal drive. The very thing that was supposed to motivate them ended up demotivating them once the monitoring for the reward disappeared (Deci & Cascio).[29]

This matters more than we realize, especially for managers. We think adding a bonus will make our team work harder, or longer, or better. And it might, for a little while. But if we're only tapping into extrinsic motivation, we're *renting* their attention instead of *earning* their engagement.

---

[29] (Deci & Cascio, 1972)

Which brings us to intrinsic motivation. The long-lasting, deeply satisfying, I-did-this-because-it-mattered-to-me kind of motivation. This type of motivation is not transactional. It's about meaning. While it might not come with a free slice of pizza, it will come with more joy, more curiosity, and a much stronger likelihood that your team will stay after the meeting to keep puzzling, even when no one's watching.

Researchers Deci, Ryan, and Flaste, two of the founding minds behind Self-Determination Theory (SDT), found that intrinsic motivation is driven by three core psychological needs: autonomy, competence, and relatedness. Autonomy is the feeling that we have control over our choices and our time. Competence is that sense of satisfaction that comes from doing something well and continuing to grow. Relatedness is the human need to feel connected to others (Deci & Flaste, 1995).[30]

These three drivers are the holy trinity of intrinsic motivation. When we create environments that nurture them, people don't only comply, they engage. They care about the work they do. If you're trying to lead humans (as opposed to robots), that's kind of the whole point. Let's take a closer look at what each of these three psychological needs look like in the workplace.

Autonomy

Autonomy is the psychological equivalent of sitting in the driver's seat with your hands on the wheel in full control of your Spotify playlist. It's the deeply human

---

[30] (Deci & Flaste, Why we do what we do: The dynamics of personal autonomy, 1995)

desire to feel like we are the ones in charge and we aren't just being dragged behind cargo.

It shows up in all kinds of ways, including the freedom to decide what we're working on, how we're tackling it, or when we'll take our lunch break. It's the difference between being asked to do something and being told what to do. When you're in a management role, your words either reinforce autonomy or strip it away.

One of my favorite studies around this very point comes from an elementary school art class. In the experiment, students in two different classrooms were given the same assignment with the same restriction. They could paint with only six different colors. The only difference was in how the instruction was delivered. In one classroom, the teacher said, "Do not mix the colors." Simple, direct, and rigid. In the other, the teacher said, "I know it would be fun to mix the colors, but if we do, the next class won't have any paint left." Same rule, with a completely different tone. One restricts, the other relates.

The students went on to complete their artwork, and then outside judges rated the work on creativity and technical merit. The students who received the autonomy-supportive instructions were rated higher across the board (Deci, Nezlek, & Sheinman, 1981).[31]

This is what it means to lead with autonomy in mind. It's not about giving your team total control over everything. It's about how you frame your ask, how you craft your systems, and whether you're thinking like the

---

[31] (Deci, Nezlek, & Sheinman, Characteristics of the rewarder and intrinsic motivation of the rewardee., 1981)

person on the receiving end or thinking like a manager with a checklist to finish.

Let me give you an example from one of my clients, an independent coffee shop. Now, in this shop, they distilled weekly updates to their staff through a word document the managers typed up. These updates were fairly short and included changes in the store hours, updates on things that had been moved in storage, and a number of other tiny but important details people needed to know to do their jobs well.

Originally, the managers wrote these updates on a document on the computer and uploaded them to the digital platform. When the employees' shift ended and they went to clock out, it would ask them to check a box confirming they'd read the update. Now, what do you think happened in this scenario? If you guessed people checked the box but *didn't* read the update, you're getting the hang of motivation theory.

It was clear we needed to change this system. It was currently designed for what was most convenient for the managers, not what was most convenient for the employees. Reading a lot of text on a word doc, on a small screen (most clocked out via a phone app) was frustrating for everyone. So, we decided to start designing it for how the employees were currently behaving.

Instead of posting it in an app, the update got printed and posted right next to the handwashing sink. At the start of every shift, each staff member was required to wash their hands. We also added stickers. A whole bucket of stickers. Once you read the update, you gave yourself a sticker on a list with all of the employees' names. A sparkly, shiny, grown-up gold star. Not only did it make the process more fun and tactile, but it created a visible, social moment. People knew who had read the update, and who didn't. It sparked conversation and it gamified the habit.

And yes, technically that sticker is an extrinsic motivator. But the design of the system came from empathy. We thought like the team, not like the management. We found a place where they go every day and stare at the wall while they wash their hands before their shift, then gave them something to look at. Getting weekly updates didn't take any additional time out of their day because they already had to be at the sink for a certain amount of time when they started their shift anyway.

That is the real takeaway here that I'd like you to remember; Autonomy isn't just a checkbox. *It's a lens*. It's a way of asking, "How do I build a system that supports someone's sense of choice and ownership, even when I'm the one setting the parameters?"

When you lead with autonomy in mind, you don't tell people what to do, you invite them into the why. You build trust, not just compliance. And maybe most importantly, you shift from managing tasks to stewarding motivation.

For me, autonomy is the umbrella over everything. It shows up in how we teach competence through supportive choice-based feedback and in how we cultivate relatedness by stepping out of the driver's seat and putting on our coaching hat (which we'll dig into later in the book). Giving autonomy doesn't mean stepping back from leadership. It means creating space for people to meet you on their terms, not dragging them into yours.

Competence

People like feeling competent. They enjoy feeling capable, effective, and a little bit badass at the thing they do. Whether it's pulling the perfect espresso shot, leading a team meeting, or running a mile without walking, we are wired to want to get better at the things we do. That internal drive to improve is a key pillar of intrinsic motivation because progress *feels good.*

When I started my sourdough journey, it was a wild ride. Weather changes, fussy starters, and several other factors made it so no two loaves came out the same. But I kept doing it because I liked learning it. There's something deeply satisfying about knowing more this week than I did last week. And that's what competence is all about— learning, growing, and having that quiet little moment of pride that says, "Hey, I'm getting better!"

Now, take that feeling and apply it to the workplace. Your people want this too. Whether they're technicians, tellers, designers, or customer service reps, they want to feel like they're improving at something meaningful. As a manager, one of the best things you can do to fuel their motivation is to design for competence.

One of my home services clients realized that their team of technicians had nowhere to grow. No seniority levels, no defined skill ladders—just "technician" as a flat title with no visible next step. Those who had been there for *years* had no way to show their seniority. That's a problem. If there's no progression and no recognition of skill mastery, motivation starts to stall. Compare that to systems where you can go from a level one technician to a level two technician and more, or you can earn badges for specialized skills. Now you've got a workforce whose titles reflect seniority and talent.

A credit union client of mine faced something similar. In a company of two hundred employees, there was limited vertical movement. This left people feeling stuck, restless, and, over time, disengaged. Even when they liked their jobs and their teams, the lack of visible growth opportunities made it harder to stay motivated. Without something to work toward, it's easy for even the best employees to start feeling like they are treading water. Over time, stagnation chips away at energy, curiosity, and pride in the work. People *need* a sense of progression, even if it's small, to keep that internal engine running.

Stagnation is the enemy of motivation. That's why great leaders create systems that acknowledge growth, whether it's formal promotions or informal titles that come with a bit of a pay bump. This vertical movement can help people stay engaged even when they're not technically moving up on the org chart. When you build pathways for learning and achievement, you are prepping people for promotions *and* creating consistent moments of satisfaction. You're fueling that inner drive that makes people want to keep showing up strong.

Let's not forget feedback. If structure is the skeleton of competence, feedback is the lifeblood. But not all feedback is created equal. Telling someone, "You steamed the milk to a hundred and three degrees, which is technically correct," is fine. But telling them, "Wow, this latte is delicious. I saw how focused you were and how much care you put into it. Thank you!" lights a whole different part of the brain. The first is about being technically correct. The second makes the person receiving the feedback feel seen and appreciated.

The research by Deci and Flaste also backs this up. In one study, medical interns who made a serious dosage mistake were more motivated to improve when feedback was given with empathy and openness, not judgment. Instead of saying, "You nearly killed someone," the attending might say, "What did it feel like when you realized what happened?" or "How can we support you in making sure this doesn't happen again?" The intern knows they messed up. They are likely to already feel stressed and shameful about that mistake. Hammering the point only shuts them down. But inviting them into reflection and learning keeps the door to growth open.

This is where the 5:1 feedback rule comes in, an idea popularized by Drs. John and Julie Gottman.[32] The rule says that you need five positive interactions for every one critical comment to maintain a healthy relationship with someone. That applies at work too, especially in management. If the only time you speak up is to correct someone, they'll start avoiding you like the HR department during layoffs. But if you regularly acknowledge effort, intention, and improvement in small ways, then when you do offer a course correction, it doesn't feel like a hammer. It feels like coaching.

Some industries, especially sales, lean hard on competition to drive motivation. The winner gets the bonus, everyone else gets a handshake. Sounds exciting on paper. But the research says this kind of setup can hurt overall motivation. When only one person wins, everyone else

---

[32] (Rusnak, 2020)

feels like a loser even if they did great. Think about Olympic silver medalists. They are literally the second-best person on Earth in their category, and people still say, "Aw, so close!" That's wild! Many feel sorry for them—and sometimes the athlete even feels sorry for themselves—because they didn't get the gold.

I don't want anyone I manage to feel like a disappointed Olympian. So, instead of one-winner competitions, I focus on team-based incentives. If the whole team hits a goal, they all get a reward. It could be a bonus, a pizza party, or anything in between, but the key is the task requires collective effort to achieve, and everyone gets celebrated for that effort. Not only does this foster collaboration, but it also protects the collective morale. It says, "We rise together," not "Only the top dog eats."

Now, let's bring in Carol Dweck's work on growth mindset. In her book *Mindset*,[33] she outlines the idea that our abilities aren't fixed. With time, energy, and effort, we can always learn and improve. She writes, "The remarkable thing I've learned from my research is that in the growth mindset, you don't always need confidence. What I mean is that even when you think you're not good at something, you can still plunge into it wholeheartedly and stick to it." This mindset has huge implications for how we lead. It teaches us the power of *yet*. "I'm not good at spreadsheets" becomes "I'm not good at spreadsheets yet." One word reframes the whole story from one of limitation to one of potential.

When you give feedback with a growth mindset, you are no longer only speaking to the result needed. Instead,

---

[33] (Dweck, 2007)

you are affirming the process. You might say, "I can see how much thought you put into the structure and design of this presentation. Thank you! With a few tweaks, I think it will be exactly what we need." That kind of feedback makes people feel seen and supported. It keeps the internal drive humming. It points to the need for improvement without dismissing the effort they've put in so far.

Whether you're a manager, a teacher, or a parent, you're in the business of shaping belief. And belief, especially belief in our own potential, is rocket fuel for intrinsic motivation.

If you want to help your people feel competent, don't just tell them what they did wrong. Tell them what they did *well*. Tell them how they're growing. Show them where they're headed. When you do offer corrections, do it with a light touch and a whole lot of "yet." When people believe they can improve, they will. They'll surprise you, and they'll probably surprise themselves too.

Relatedness

In the scientific literature, this third pillar of intrinsic motivation is called "relatedness," but in everyday terms, it comes down to the question *Do I like this person?* Whether it's your teacher, manager, coworker, or teammate, that quiet internal question matters. Research shows that when we feel connected to someone, we're more likely to be motivated, engaged, and willing to do the hard stuff, even when there's no gold star in sight.[34]

Look, I know some old-school managers will say, "It doesn't matter if my employees like me." Okay. Sure. You

---

[34] (Quintero, 2014)

can keep that flag flying if you want. But I'd invite you to consider this: What if being liked isn't only about popularity? What if it unlocks better performance? Because it does. People work harder, communicate better, and show up more fully when they feel connected to you and to each other.

So how do we build that connection? You won't do it with forced fun or mandatory trust falls. (Please, no more of these.) We build rapport through attentiveness, shared experiences, basic human kindness, humor, and transparency. In short, by being a person and not a management bot.

One of the simplest ways to build that connection is by making space for small, consistent moments of sharing. If you have recurring team meetings, try starting each one with a quick round of "highs and lows" or "roses and thorns" or "happies and crappies." Invite each person to share one good thing and one hard thing from their week. They get to decide how personal or professional they want to be. Over time, you'll notice that most people gravitate toward sharing family updates, weekend wins, or personal stressors. That's not a distraction. That's the good stuff. When people feel safe enough to show up as their whole selves, connection deepens, and so does collaboration.

This same principle applies in leadership. You don't have to share your deepest secrets at the Monday morning meeting. You don't need a weekly "Feelings Circle." But you do need to show your people that you're human. Talk about your Trader Joe's obsession. Mention your weekend hike. Celebrate their small wins and remember their dog's name. These tiny acts of connection create the psychological glue that keeps teams motivated and collaborative.

Another large piece of this is how your team feels about each other. One of the findings in my dissertation was that students who felt connected to their instructors reported higher levels of learning and motivation.[35] Why? Because you learn more from someone you trust, and you take more risks when your leader makes you feel safe.

That means managers don't just need strong individual relationships with team members, but we also need to cultivate team cohesion. Block time on your calendar for team building, even if it's low-key. Get everyone in a room without an agenda once in a while. Bake connection into the culture, not just the one on ones. We'll talk more about how to do this in our upcoming leadership hat chapter.

I saw this play out in a nonprofit I volunteer with each year. Every new class runs a fundraiser, and honestly, it's usually a little pricey. This year, I didn't have a burning reason to go or any major social obligation. But I went anyway, because I wanted to show the team that I support them. I wanted to be someone who shows up. I went, chatted, had a glass of wine, participated in the silent auction, and showed them how much I appreciated their hard work by enjoying the event alongside them. It would have been easy for me to stay home and be a couch potato—who doesn't love that?—but I would have missed an opportunity to build the relationship between myself and the team.

Relatedness creates a sense of responsibility too. When you care about the people around you, you feel more

---

[35] (Ryan & Wilson, 2014)

accountable for the whole. You *want* to carry your weight so the team doesn't have to carry it for you. This is how relatedness drives performance.

So, if you're in the business of managing people, you're also in the business of building relationships. And I mean real relationships, not performative ones. As we'll explore in the next chapter, vulnerability is part of this too. But for now, know this connection isn't a distraction from work. *It is the work.*

Intrinsic Is the Long Game

By now, you can probably see that motivation isn't a one-size-fits-all formula. As managers, we've got a full toolbox available to us. Yes, extrinsic motivators have their place. Bonuses, perks, and pizza parties are not evil. They're tools. Like any tool, they can be useful if you know when and how to use them. But they aren't the long-term solution.

If you want sustainable performance, lasting growth, and a team that exceeds expectations, you've got to use the three pillars of motivation theory to build systems that support intrinsic motivation. That's where the real power lies. Lucky for us, it's also the space we have the most influence over.

Intrinsic motivation starts with relationships. It shows up in the way we give feedback, the trust we build, and the roles and responsibilities we design to help people grow. It's woven into how we connect with others, how we create a sense of belonging, and how we invite people to care about more than just the work in front of them. Like anything meaningful, it's a practice.

You won't get it perfect. The culture will shift, the generations will change, and what works now may not work forever. But the core truth—that humans want to feel autonomous, competent, and connected—will stay the same. We *want* to matter, and when we do, we work better, and we live better.

As you move forward in your role, remember that motivation isn't something you force. It's something you foster. The more human you are in that process, the more your team will rise to meet you.

If motivation is the engine, then values are the map. You can't build lasting motivation—let alone a cohesive, high-functioning team—without knowing what you stand for. Your team's values determine which behaviors get rewarded, which decisions get made, and what kind of energy fuels your culture. So, before you can foster motivation that sticks, you've got to get clear on the principles that guide you. That's where we're headed next.

Chapter 6:
The Values That Ground You

For years, corporate America has been obsessed with mission and vision statements. I'm sure you've seen them before. They are the carefully curated, poster-worthy phrases meant to inspire action usually displayed on the wall. While they serve a purpose, mission and vision statements don't shape how decisions are made, how teams function, or which behaviors get rewarded. That is where values come in.

Values are "we are" statements that guide your team's behavior, shape your leadership style, and define the energy of your organization. When high-functioning teams build decision-making around shared values, they perform better, communicate better, and retain employees longer. But when values are unclear—or nonexistent—companies end up hiring people who simply don't fit.

I once worked with a business that valued inclusivity, cooperation, and relationships. They built their entire company culture around the idea that people work best together. Then they hired someone who valued radical independence and actively disliked collaboration. They had no interest in building relationships and preferred working in isolation.

From day one, this employee clashed with the team. They dismissed brainstorming sessions, avoided social interactions, and resisted any feedback that required a shift in approach. It became a massive energy drain on the business. Months later, leadership found themselves trying to navigate how to get this person out of the company, a costly and exhausting process that could have been avoided entirely had they simply prioritized values from the start.

Unfortunately, this isn't an isolated incident. I see it happen all the time. Companies obsess over résumés and skill sets while completely ignoring whether a candidate actually *vibes* with how they operate. The fallout creates expensive turnover and team drama that makes reality TV look tame. Which leaves managers stuck in an endless loop of playing therapist, referee, and cleanup crew all at the same time. If you don't define the energy you want to work in (aka, your values), you are sending out an open invitation for the wrong employees, the wrong clients, and the wrong business opportunities to waltz right in and make themselves at home.

Luckily, defining values doesn't have to be complicated. In fact, it shouldn't be. But many organizations overcomplicate it with corporate jargon and bloated sentences like:

> *We strive for kindness and compassion in all that we do while uplifting those around us with unwavering integrity and purpose.*

Sure, this sounds pretty, but what does it truly mean? Instead of long, poetic statements, strong values should be simple, singular words that capture the essence of what your business stands for. Five is a good number. Not five phrases. Not five ideas squished into a single sentence. Five words.

For example, my personal values are:

- Adventure
- Lifelong learning
- Mental wellness
- Physical wellness
- Community

When I live in alignment with these values, I'm at my best. When I don't, things start feeling off. The same applies to your business. Your values should be clear enough that they actively shape decision-making, from the people you hire to the way you structure meetings, approach conflict, and set goals. If they don't, they're just decoration.

If your organization hasn't nailed down its values yet, or if they are collecting dust in a forgotten mission statement that no one follows, don't panic. You can start right where you are. Even if you're not calling the shots for the whole company, you can define the values for your team. Figure out what matters in how you work together, make those values loud and clear, and start bringing in people who get it.

When discussing values, it's important to note we have personal values, and organizations can have organizational values. If you're a CEO and haven't yet defined organizational values, I highly recommend bringing in a professional to help with this process. Organizational values are such complex driving forces that it is worth investing in some help to make sure you get it right. As for personal values, that's a journey you can explore without an expert around.

Discover Your Personal Core Values

No values are *bad* values. This is the first thing I tell my clients when we start this exercise. Whether you're identifying values for yourself or your organization, the goal isn't to judge what's "good" or "bad," it's to find what's true for you.

Now, all values are universally positive attributes. They include words like honesty, courage, respect, innovation, and compassion. They represent shared moral agreements, the traits we admire in others, and the qualities we strive to live by. But just because a value is inherently good doesn't mean it belongs on your personal list.

Take honesty, for example. Most people would say it's a great value to have. And I agree, it is. But for me, honesty has been a source of pain. I've had experiences where honesty was used as a weapon, where people framed their harsh words as "just being honest" without any regard for kindness or impact. Because of this, honesty isn't in my top values. It's what I call a shadow value—a concept we'll get into later.

For now, let's focus on discovering the values that resonate most deeply with you.

How to Identify Your Personal Core Values

Whether you're exploring your personal values, guiding a team toward a shared vision, or defining the foundational principles of a business, this exercise is a powerful tool for clarity and alignment.

You can do this exercise alone for some self-discovery, with a team to create a shared vision (and fewer passive-aggressive emails), or as a business strategy session to ensure your company stands for something beyond quarterly profits. However you use it, expect some light existential questioning, a few "aha" moments, and maybe even a realization or two about why certain things at work drive you absolutely insane.

Step 1: Sort Your Values

For this exercise, I like the PEAK Values Card Deck[36] which contains fifty-eight cards. In the workshops I run, I have members sort through this deck. Each card has a value on it with a sentence or two describing what that value means. I have them short these values into four piles:

- Yes—Values that immediately feel right.
- No—Values that don't resonate or feel important to you.
- Maybe—Values that you're drawn to but aren't sure if they're top-tier.
- Ick—Values that rub you the wrong way.

Once you have your Yes Pile, you'll likely have around ten or twenty words. The challenge now is to cut it to your top five. This is *not* about choosing what sounds nice. It's about identifying the values that define who you are at your core. The ones that make you say, "hell yes!", and when you live in alignment with them, they make you feel fulfilled, energized, and whole.

---

[36] (The PEAK Fleet, n.d.)

Step 2: Align Your Values with Your Work and Life

Now that you have your top values, take a step back and ask:

- How does my work align with these values?
- How does my personal life reflect them?
- Am I surrounding myself with people (friends, colleagues, mentors) who share these values?

PEAK VALUES CARDS

Our values drive our behaviors, thoughts, and decisions. If you're feeling drained, stuck, or out of sync in your career or relationships, there's a good chance your environment isn't aligned with your values.

If you don't have access to these cards, here is a table with forty values you can review to help define your personal values:

- Authority: To be in charge of and responsible for others
- Autonomy: To have independence and self-determination
- Ecology: To live in harmony with the environment
- Challenge: To take on difficult tasks and problems
- Philanthropy: To be of service to others
- Adventure: To seek out new and unknown experiences
- Creativity: To have new and original ideas
- Dependability: To be reliable and trustworthy
- Change: To have a full life of change and variety

- Comfort: To have a pleasant and comfortable life
- Commitment: To make enduring, meaningful commitments
- Compassion: To feel and act on concern for others
- Friendship: To have close, supportive friends
- Excitement: To have a life full of thrills and stimulation
- Flexibility: To adjust to new circumstances easily
- Family: To have a happy, loving family
- Respect: The consideration of others as equals
- Stability: To have a life that stays fairly consistent
- Mindfulness: To live conscious and mindful of the present moment
- Leisure: To take time to relax and enjoy
- Fun: To play and have fun
- Generosity: To give what I have to others
- Authenticity: To act in a manner that is true to who I am
- Growth: To keep changing and growing
- Tradition: To embody a way(s) of life given to us by our ancestors
- Simplicity: To live life simply, with minimal needs
- Mental Wellness: To be spiritually well and healthy
- Physical Wellness: To be physically well and healthy
- Honesty: To be honest and truthful
- Optimism: To maintain a positive and optimistic outlook
- Humility: To be modest and unassuming
- Humor: To see the humorous side of myself and the world
- Inner Peace: To experience personal peace

- Intimacy: To share my innermost experiences with others
- Justice: To promote fair and equal treatment
- Open-Mindedness: To be open to new experiences, ideas and options
- Organization: To have a life that is well-ordered and organized
- Spirituality: To grow and mature spiritually
- Rationality: To be guided by reason and logic
- Responsibility: To make and carry out responsible decisions

Do Our Values Ever Change?

For the most part, no, our values don't change. We evolve as humans, but our core values tend to stay the same because they are part of what makes us who we are. For example, one of my core values is community. How that plays out in my life has changed over the years. But my need for connection has never wavered. It's the foundation of who I am.

That said, life events can be catalysts for shifting values. A major personal loss, a career change, or another big life event could bring certain values to the forefront that weren't as strong before. But overall, our values are what anchor us and typically stay the same throughout our lives.

This is why hiring people whose values align with your organization is critical. Skills can be taught and processes can be learned, but values are deeply ingrained. They are the operating systems that run in the background of every decision a person makes. When you bring someone onto your team who doesn't share your core values, you're inviting long-term friction.

Think of it like hiring someone who technically knows how to row but prefers to paddle in their own rhythm while your whole team is synchronized. Sure, they might adjust for a while, but eventually, they'll either burn out from trying to fit in or unintentionally throw everyone else off course. On the flip side, when values align, it's effortless. You don't have to constantly course correct or remind someone why certain things matter because they already *get* it. That's the kind of alignment that makes teams stronger.

Now, this doesn't mean every employee has to share all of your company's values. But if there's no overlap at all between your company's values and personal values, that's where tension and conflict will come in. If someone aligns with two or three of your company's values, they'll likely feel connected to the culture and thrive there.

Don't Forget Shadow Values

These are "ick" values that hit a nerve (those in the fourth pile). If it stirs up a strong emotional reaction, like honesty does for me, set it aside. These are often shadow values, and we'll unpack them here.

Not all values sit comfortably with us. Some push our buttons in ways we can't quite explain. They feel *off*, even though, on the surface, they are positive qualities. These are what I call shadow values.

A shadow value isn't bad. It's a value that, for whatever reason, hits a nerve. Maybe it reminds you of a past experience, or it represents something you've struggled with. Maybe it's been used against you. It might even be something you admire in others but feel resistant to embracing yourself.

For me, independence is a shadow value. I admire independent people. I understand why autonomy is important. But when a group places too much emphasis on independence, I feel uneasy. I've been in environments where my need for collaboration was seen as a weakness, where I was excluded because I wasn't "independent enough." So now, when I'm in a space where independence is the dominant value, I don't feel safe. I feel like I have to fight for my place.

Let's go back to honesty. That shadow value took me years to unpack. I absolutely choose to be honest, but my personal experiences have made me wary of the way honesty can be wielded. I've seen people use honesty as a blunt-force weapon, treating cruelty as a virtue just because it's "the truth." I've been on the receiving end of people who pride themselves on brutal honesty, only to leave a wake of hurt feelings and unnecessary conflict behind them. So, while I value honesty, I place kindness above it. I don't believe in radical transparency. I believe in truth with care and nuance.

That's the thing about shadow values. They don't always make logical sense. They're emotional. Sometimes, they come with a gut reaction you don't understand at first. Maybe you see a value on someone else's list and feel your nose wrinkle, or you hear someone talk about how much they value something, and it sparks resistance in you. You might even feel a little judgmental and think, *Why would someone value that so much?* That's your cue to dig deeper.

For years, I struggled with my reaction to honesty. I knew it was a good thing. But it still hit a nerve. It wasn't until I took a step back that I understood it wasn't honesty itself that bothered me, but it was my experiences with it. Specifically, experiences where honesty was used in a way that felt weaponized, cold, or unkind. That distinction matters. Because now, instead of rejecting honesty altogether, I can articulate how I value it differently.

That is the real power of understanding shadow values. They help you understand yourself *and* help you navigate why other people might approach the world differently than you do.

How Shadow Values Create Conflict

Most workplace conflict doesn't happen because someone is wrong. It happens because values clash. Take my example with honesty. If I'm on a team with someone who values absolute transparency, who doesn't want to "sugarcoat" their words and believes in offering full clarity at all times even if it hurts someone's feelings, I likely won't work well with them.

Of course, this goes both ways. The hyper-honest person might see me as too cautious or too careful with my words. They might even think I'm being dishonest because I don't immediately blurt out everything I think. I, on the other hand, might see them as harsh, reckless, and insensitive because they don't take the time to soften their delivery—much like a human bullhorn with no volume control. Neither of us is wrong. But our values are naturally competing, and if we don't recognize that, it's going to create unnecessary tension.

This kind of value clash shows up in teams all the time. Someone who thrives on collaboration might struggle in a workplace that champions independence. A manager who values flexibility might butt heads with an employee who craves structure. Someone who moves fast and values quick execution will constantly feel frustrated by a team member who values thoroughness and precision, and vice versa.

Most of the time, these conflicts aren't about competence. It's not that someone *can't* do the job, it's that their *way* of doing things makes you want to scream into a pillow. And that's usually not because they are wrong, but because they see the world through a completely different lens. The two of you are in a misalignment.

This is why understanding shadow values is so important. If a certain value rubs you the wrong way, don't assume that person is the absolute worst. Instead, take a step back and ask why it's hitting a nerve. If you recognize that a teammate holds a value which directly contradicts one of yours, you can start seeing it as a difference in perspective rather than a personal attack.

As a leader, this awareness is gold. Instead of assuming an employee is difficult or uncooperative, you can look at how their values align or don't align with the role they're in. If you have someone who hates collaboration, don't force them into a team-heavy environment. Instead, find ways for them to work more independently. If someone thrives on structured processes, don't expect them to excel in a "figure-it-out-as-you-go" culture.

When we take the time to understand values, both in ourselves and in others, we reduce conflict and build stronger, more aligned teams. Which, let's be honest, means fewer passive-aggressive comments and a lot less teeth-gritting meetings.

When You Don't Live Your Values

Not living your values is a bit like walking around in an ill-fitting costume playing a role that just isn't you. When we live out of alignment with our values, our brains and bodies throw up red flags. We feel anxiety, burnout, and that nagging feeling of *what am I even doing with my life?* Frustration spikes, and suddenly, we're doom-scrolling job listings (or Instagram reels) in the middle of the night.

But living against our values is worse. That's when every task feels like pulling teeth, and we start questioning whether we've been gaslighting ourselves into thinking we care about this at all. It's the creeping dread on Sunday night, the constant mental negotiation (*Do I really need this job? Could I live off-grid with a few goats?*), and the exhaustion that no amount of PTO ever seems to fix.

The friction of misaligned values is draining. It seeps into everything. You'll find yourself procrastinating on tasks you once enjoyed and feeling oddly resentful toward coworkers who seem totally fine. The worst part is that no amount of skill or competence can fix it. If your core values aren't reflected in your job, it's like trying to fit a square peg into a round hole. Sure, you can shove it in there with enough force, but at what cost? Hint: probably your sanity.

Typically, when we are misaligned, we see conflicts in business and our interpersonal relationships. You might see these types of values clash when it comes to organization as well. If you run an event planning business built around meticulous organization and structured step-by-step systems, then hire someone who thrives in the chaos, it simply won't work out. No matter how charismatic they were in the interview or how much experience they might have in the industry.

That's not to say every job needs to align perfectly with your values. A paycheck is a paycheck, and sometimes we take jobs just to cover the bills. That's fine. But if you're in a role that actively contradicts your core values, that's when the slow soul-suck begins. If you need to stay in a job like that, make sure you're finding other ways to live your values outside of work, and start looking for an exit plan. Life's too short for that kind of existential misery.

Another thing to keep in mind: Familiarity isn't the same as alignment. You can have a deep personal history with someone and still find yourself clashing at work. Hiring a family member or working with a close friend sounds like a great idea, until it's not. Just because you grew up together or have years of history doesn't mean you're aligned on what matters most in a work setting. When values clash, tensions rise fast. The same goes for romantic relationships. If you get together with someone because they're convenient (i.e., they live five minutes away and your mutual friend sets you up), but you don't share core values, you're setting yourself up for friction.

Now, conflict happens. It's inevitable. Even when we do share values, we'll still butt heads because we all have different experiences and perspectives. But when we *know* where those differences lie, we can meet each other halfway. Values alignment doesn't mean total agreement. It means awareness, compromise, and ensuring that the core of your work, relationships, and daily life support who you are at your core.

Value-Focused Hiring

Hiring for values doesn't mean creating a cookie-cutter team of people who think, act, and look the same. That's not a team; that's an echo chamber. You *want* diversity. You *need* diversity. Different backgrounds and experiences are what fuels creativity and problem-solving. But at the core, your team should share the same foundational values, the big non-negotiables that drive your business forward.

Here are a few key steps to follow when hiring with values in mind:

Step 1: Know Your Organization's Values

Before you can hire people who align with your company values, you need to know what they are. That means getting crystal clear on what your company stands for and how those values show up in daily work. Once you have that figured out, say it in the job posting, loud and clear.

Example: "We value radical transparency, collaboration, and accountability. We hire people who live these values. If this doesn't sound like you, please don't apply."

Being upfront about your values in the job description attracts the right people—those who read it and think, "Hell yes! This is my kind of place." It weeds out the wrong people before they even submit an application.

Step 2: Look for Values in the Résumé

When reviewing résumés, most people focus on skills and experience. That's important, but I also assess values alignment, which I use as its own category in the hiring rubric.

Ask yourself:

- Do they mention our values in their experience?
- Do their past roles reflect values that align with our organization?
- Does their cover letter give any insight into what they care about beyond "I need a job"?

If I see zero connection between their résumé and our values, that's a red flag. It doesn't necessarily mean they are a bad candidate, but it does mean they might not be a fit for our team culture.

Step 3: Make Values Part of the Interview

Once candidates make it to the interview, have scenario-based questions prepared that will reveal how they think. Instead of asking about a time they worked well on a team (which is entirely too vague), offer a real-world situation they will likely face in the role.

For example, in a coffee shop where teamwork and initiative are core values, I might say, "You're working a busy Saturday shift. You've been on the register for hours, and now you want to switch to the bar. How do you handle the transition?"

Their response tells me everything. If they say, "I'd tell my coworker it's time to switch," and that's how we do things here? Great. If they hesitate, overcomplicate it, or struggle to see the importance of smooth transitions in a fast-paced environment? They might not be a fit.

Step 4: Spot-Check in the First Six Months

When someone is new to our organization, we need to be sure they are actually a fit. That's why I keep an eye on new hires for the first few months. Not to micromanage, but to see if their actions align with their words.

- Are they embodying the values they claimed to have in the interview?
- Are their teammates eager to work with them, or do people ask not to be scheduled with them?
- Do they naturally contribute to the team culture, or are they low-key disrupting it?

This isn't about nitpicking; it's about making sure everyone is in the right place. If someone's values don't align, it's not a personal failure. It's a mismatch. That type of misalignment will quickly become apparent within the first few months.

Step 5: Address Misalignment Early

When a new hire clearly isn't a fit for the culture, I don't drag things out. I'm not a fan of long performance improvement plans (PIPs) when the issue is about deeper misalignment because core beliefs and behaviors don't usually shift overnight (or at all).

Instead, I focus on behavioral expectations. I might say, "Here's what alignment with our values looks like in action. Can you meet these expectations?"

If they can't, or simply don't want to, then it's in everyone's best interest to help them move on. Not in a cold, cutthroat way, but in a "let's find you a place where you'll actually thrive" kind of way. If they are struggling, chances are they aren't happy either, and no one wants to feel like the odd one out.

Step 6: Keep Values Conversations Alive

Even when you have built a team full of people who share core values, you need to keep the conversation going. That way everyone gets a consistent reminder of how best to work with those on the team. I like to do this through team value-sharing exercise:

- Have team members share their personal values and how they align with the company's values.
- Ask each individual to share their shadow values.
- Encourage open conversations about how values influence decision-making, collaboration, and conflict resolution.

By creating space for these discussions, you're reinforcing alignment while allowing individuals to bring their full selves to work.

Fewer Values, Stronger Direction

On a final note, keep in mind: If you (or your organization) have too many values, they stop being values and start being confetti. Scattered. Unfocused. A whole lot of movement with no real direction.

I once had a client who wanted twelve organizational values. *Twelve*. That's not a guiding framework, that's a manifesto. A boat can't point in twelve directions at once. If you're steering a company, a team, or even your own career, you need a clear course. Otherwise, you're just paddling in circles.

So, how many values should you have? I believe five is the magic number. They should be your "hell yes!" values. If a value doesn't make you want to plant your flag and rally your people, let it go.

That doesn't mean the values you don't choose aren't good values. It also doesn't mean you don't value them. They just might not be the core of your organization. Maybe they're guiding principles, maybe they're personal beliefs, or maybe they influence your culture in a more subtle way. But if they don't shape the direction of your team, they don't need to be on the list. And that's okay!

So, as you wrap up this exercise, ask yourself:
- Are these values clear enough to guide decisions?
- Do they reflect who we are at our core, not just who we wish we were?
- Could I explain each of these values in a single, punchy sentence?

If the answer is yes, you're good. If not, it's time to cut the fluff. When your values are sharp, focused, and true, they drive everything forward.

Once your values are clear, you have a compass. You're not only steering strategy, you're leading people. People with histories. People with triggers. People whose past experiences shape how they show up at work, even if they never say a word about it. That's why trauma-informed management is a core part of modern leadership. To truly lead with empathy and effectiveness, you need to understand the invisible baggage your team may be carrying.

Chapter 7:

Trauma-Informed Management

If you've never heard of the Adverse Childhood Experiences (ACE) Scale, buckle up, because it's essentially a scorecard for how much childhood turbulence you survived. It's been around since 1998 and has been widely used in research to measure the long-term impact of childhood trauma on health, behavior, and, as you might guess, the way we show up in adulthood, including at work.

The ACE scale measures ten different types of childhood adversity, including physical abuse, emotional neglect, and growing up in a household where addiction or mental illness was present. Your score can range from zero to ten, with zero meaning you had the childhood equivalent of a Disney movie (before the tragic parent death scene) and ten meaning…well, you deserve a hug and possibly a therapy dog.

The higher your ACE score, the more challenging life tends to be. People with an ACE score of four or higher are significantly more likely to struggle with mental health challenges, substance abuse, and even chronic illness.[37] Those with a six or higher have an average lifespan that's nearly twenty years shorter.[38] Let that sink in. Two decades shaved off a life, not because of choices, but because of childhood circumstances entirely outside their control.

But here's where things get even more fascinating and mildly unsettling. Trauma doesn't just live in our

---

[37] (Broekhof, Nordahl, Tanum, & Selvik, 2023)
[38] (What ACEs do you have?, n.d.)

memories. It gets passed down. If your parents were anxious, stressed, or operating in survival mode, there's a good chance that wiring got handed down to you, literally. Science has shown that trauma can be encoded in our genes, meaning that even if you grew up in a peaceful, low-drama home, you might still carry some of that inherited anxiety or hypervigilance from previous generations.

So, why does this matter in the workplace? Because the quantity of adverse experiences a person has isn't just a health issue, it's a performance issue. People who carry trauma often experience chronic stress, difficulty with emotional regulation, and heightened sensitivity to conflict or criticism. That means a simple "Hey, can we talk?" from a boss might trigger a fight-or-flight response in an employee whose nervous system has been conditioned to expect the worst.

The good news? Research shows that having one caring, stable relationship in childhood can work like a psychological life raft, dramatically improving long-term outcomes for people who have faced adversity. A single reliable mentor, coach, or teacher can be the difference between someone spiraling into a mess of bad decisions or figuring out how to thrive.

If one safe person can change the course of someone's entire life, *imagine* what a trauma-informed manager can do.

Unpacking the Weight We Carry

By the time we enter the workplace, most of us are already carrying more than a laptop and a to-do list. We bring our pasts with us, including our upbringing, our attachments, our wounds, and our traumas. Whether we know it or not, that history shapes how we show up. One of the best metaphors I've found for this is the trauma suitcase. It's a mental and emotional carry-on we all lug around. What's inside may differ, but the impact is universal. If we want to lead well, we should get curious about what's in our own bag and what might be in the bags of the people we manage.

No two suitcases are the same. Some are heavy, some are barely zipped shut, and some people have learned to carry theirs so quietly you'd never guess it was there at all. If you grew up in a home with two stable adults who prioritized your well-being, your suitcase might be on the lighter side. Maybe you had consistent meals, a safe place to sleep, and people who showed up for you. Especially if you lived in a first-world country with reliable utilities, access to healthcare, and a stable education system. Those things make a difference. The more basic needs we have met, the lighter our emotional suitcase tends to be. But if you didn't have those things growing up, your trauma suitcase will be much heavier.

By the time we are twelve months old, our brains have already been wired with an attachment style.[39] Before we even have words, we're learning how to connect with the world based on how the people around us show up...or don't.

DISCOVER YOUR ATTACHMENT STYLE

---

[39] (Graham, 2008)

- Secure attachment? You had multiple caregivers who consistently met your needs. You learned that people are reliable, and you approach relationships with trust.
- Avoidant attachment? Maybe caregivers were physically present but emotionally distant. You learned that you had to be self-sufficient, that relying on others wasn't always safe.
- Anxious attachment? Maybe love and care felt inconsistent. Sometimes it was there, sometimes it wasn't, so you learned to be hyper-aware of people's moods, trying to control the uncontrollable.

If you don't know your personal attachment style, you can take a free test at quiz.attachmentproject.com. It's a helpful tool because how we were cared for as infants wires how we connect with others as adults. That wiring shapes how we lead, how we respond to stress, and how we handle conflict. It becomes part of the emotional baggage we carry into every workplace, interaction, and decision. And that's just our *starting* suitcase.

Life keeps adding to it. The first eighteen years of life pack a lot into that bag. Then as an adult, we continually keep stuffing it with trauma-filled experiences. Global pandemics? Throw some extra weight in. Getting bullied? More weight. A traumatic event like an accident, a betrayal, or a sudden loss? That's another weight added. Life keeps tossing more weight in, whether we want it to or not.

As adults, it's on us to figure out what's in our suitcase and decide what we want to keep carrying. Some things we can unpack, work through, and lighten. Usually with therapy. Others might have to stay, but our awareness of them makes them easier to manage. Of course, knowing what's in our bag doesn't mean it disappears; it just means we can stop pretending it's not there and become more aware of how that weight affects our day-to-day interactions.

When it comes to how we manage, we tend to lead with our suitcase. Especially if we haven't addressed anything within that suitcase. Our past shows up in our management style, and if we are carrying a heavy bag filled with unresolved stress, unchecked biases, or our own fears, it will impact how we lead.

On top of that, everyone on our team has a suitcase, too. As managers, part of our job is recognizing that people aren't just reacting to the stress in front of them, but they are also reacting through the lens of everything they have been through. Their responses are shaped by the weight they've been carrying, often without realizing it. If we're not aware of that, we risk misreading behavior, making assumptions, or mishandling tough conversations.

What People Think Trauma Is

When people hear the word *trauma*, they tend to picture something catastrophic, like war veterans struggling with PTSD or survivors of devastating car crashes. Yes, those are big traumatic experiences, but they aren't the only kinds of trauma. Trauma can happen in small moments as well.

It can look like receiving a steady stream of angry emails from a boss, each one triggering anxiety and making work feel unsafe. It can be a leader standing in front of their team and saying, "If you don't want to be on this train, get off," making it clear that speaking up or questioning decisions could cost you your job. It can be the slow erosion of confidence caused by a manager who only acknowledges mistakes and never successes. Sure, trauma can be large, like someone trying to run you off the road, but it can also be as subtle as the moments that shake our sense of self, our identity, or our ability to trust others.

The real challenge of trauma isn't just what happens in the moment—it's what lingers afterward. It can feel like someone took an eggbeater to your brain, scrambling your sense of safety and leaving you on high alert. The brain, always focused on survival, locks onto that fear and goes into defense mode. Rational thought takes a backseat while the nervous system takes over, pushing us into fight, flight, freeze, or fawn.

Which means that at its core, trauma is anything that pushes the brain out of its natural rhythm, shifting it from thinking mode into survival mode. A person who expects to feel respected at work but is publicly humiliated by a colleague is experiencing a disruption. Someone who has always felt financially stable but suddenly loses their job is experiencing a disruption. A manager who has trusted their team implicitly but is blindsided by a betrayal is experiencing a disruption. These moments shake us, affecting how we move forward, how we lead, and how we interact with others.

Now, we have all experienced trauma in some way, and we will experience trauma again in the future. That is part of the human experience. The real work, both for ourselves and as managers, is in recognizing when our brains are stuck in survival mode and figuring out how to bring them back down to Earth. Because staying in that space—constantly on edge, constantly defensive—impacts how safe or unsafe we make the people around us feel.

PTSD, CPTSD, and That Pesky Anxiety Gremlin

Trauma comes in different flavors, and according to the DSM-5 (the mental health field's official playbook),[40] there are two main types: the classic *one-and-done* trauma, which causes the better known PTSD, and the continuous trauma, which causes its messier, more insidious cousin, Complex PTSD (CPTSD).

PTSD is the one people are generally familiar with. It's the kind that comes from a singular, life-altering event like surviving a car crash, experiencing an assault, or, in the case of many veterans, enduring the horrors of war. It's a moment so intense that the brain slams the panic button, and from then on, it files that moment under *DO NOT FORGET OR YOU MIGHT DIE.*

Years later, the body can still react like the event is happening all over again. An adult who was attacked by a dog when they were six might still tense up at the sight of a friendly golden retriever. A veteran who lived through combat might wake up in the middle of the night to the slow rotation of ceiling fan blades and feel like they are back in a war zone, adrenaline surging as if they were under attack. The body remembers, even when logic says there's no threat.

---

[40] (Mr Ed's Circle of Trust, n.d.)

But if PTSD is a single thunderclap, CPTSD is the constant, low rumble of an incoming storm that never fully clears. It wasn't even diagnosable until recently, despite the fact that it's alarmingly common. CPTSD comes from years of consistent stress, instability, neglect, or harm. Having CPTSD is really just a polite way of saying, "Congratulations, you've unlocked the long-term subscription version of trauma!"

This is the kind of trauma that forms when childhood is a minefield of unpredictability. When caregivers were sometimes present, sometimes absent, sometimes loving, and sometimes cruel. It's the brain learning that safety isn't guaranteed, that emotional whiplash is normal, that trust is a gamble. Then, because the brain is fantastic at adapting, it wires itself accordingly. Even when life becomes stable later on, the body stays on high alert, convinced danger is right around the corner. The result is a mind that churns out worst-case scenarios, a nervous system that jumps at loud noises, and a constant, nagging sense that something is off, even when everything is objectively fine.

People with CPTSD often find that crowded rooms feel overwhelming, loud environments drain them, and too much stimulation can send them straight into sensory overload. Sleep becomes both a necessity and a battleground because while the body desperately needs rest, the mind isn't always willing to let its guard down. And then there's the anxiety gremlin whispering worst-case scenarios, second-guessing every interaction, and convincing them that danger is lurking in the most mundane places.

A book published in 2024 by Stephanie Foo titled *What My Bones Know*[41] offers a raw, firsthand account of a journalist navigating her CPTSD diagnosis and the ways it played out in her work and relationships. It's a beautifully written book. If you're interested in understanding how this kind of trauma rewires a person's life, it is worth a read. The first third details the trauma itself, but if that's too much, feel free to skip ahead to part two, where she starts to unravel and heal from it. Because healing *is* possible. It takes time, patience, and a whole lot of self-awareness.

How Trauma Rewires the Nervous System

Trauma doesn't only live in memories. It sets up shop in the nervous system, rearranges the furniture, and changes the way we react to the world.

With PTSD, it's like having a hair-trigger alarm system that goes off at the slightest hint of danger, except the "danger" could be a noise, a phrase, or even something as small as a visual cue. A person who has been rear-ended in traffic might spend months checking their rearview mirror with the hyper-focus of a hawk, convinced that every car approaching from behind is about to slam into them. Someone who lived through an emergency plane landing isn't exactly going to be whistling and relaxed on their next flight; they'll be gripping the armrests and praying that the laws of aerodynamics hold steady. That anxious, gut-wrenching feeling? That's the nervous system

---

[41] (Foo, 2023`)

on high alert, convinced that history is about to repeat itself.

CPTSD, on the other hand, doesn't just *activate* the nervous system, it physically changes the brain. The amygdala, the brain's fear center, gets bigger and stronger, making emotional reactions more intense.[42] The hippocampus, which is responsible for memory and emotional regulation, actually shrinks, making it harder to distinguish between past trauma and present reality.[43] This leads to a body that stays on constant alert, even when there's no immediate danger. Sleep becomes a struggle, immune systems weaken, and the body starts treating everyday stress like it's a life-threatening emergency.

For many people, CPTSD goes undiagnosed for years. Decades, even. Because unlike PTSD, which often stems from one identifiable moment, CPTSD is a slow burn, developed over years of instability, neglect, or psychological warfare.

I have CPTSD, and for me the signs were there long before I knew what to call it. I grew up in a house where no one hit me. I had clothes, food in the pantry, and two parents who, on paper, said they loved me. And yet, something always felt *off*. It wasn't until my 30s that I started putting the pieces together. First, I realized one parent's behavior was driven by addiction, then later I uncovered that the other wasn't just narcissistic, but an actual sociopath. It took years of self-exploration (and a small library of books on toxic behavior patterns) before I could see how my childhood had wired me to seek out

---

[42] (Javanbakht & Saab, 2017)
[43] (Xie & al, 2017)

people just like them. I was constantly choosing partners who mirrored those same dynamics and falling into familiar but harmful patterns, mistaking chaos for normalcy.

The realization was both validating and infuriating. I wasn't imagining things. I wasn't broken. My brain had simply been trained for survival in an unpredictable environment, and I had been carrying that wiring into adulthood without realizing it.

Healing, of course, is another beast entirely. For me, one of the biggest game-changers was a device called an Apollo wristband,[44] a small gadget that vibrates gently against my wrist, sending signals to my nervous system that I'm safe. The vibrations are so subtle that I don't consciously register them, but my heart rate slows, my sleep improves, and my body finally gets the memo that I'm not in danger. It's a tiny thing, but when you have spent your life operating in a constant state of alert, small shifts make a world of difference.

Self-Awareness, Not Armchair Diagnosis

Before you go running off to diagnose your entire team with CPTSD, take a breath. That's not your job. Your job, first and foremost, is to take care of yourself. Be aware of your own patterns, your own reactions, and where your past might be shaping your present. If anything in this chapter made something deep in your brain whisper, *huh… maybe I should look into that,* then do it. Dig into your experiences and notice where certain behaviors, fears, or patterns keep showing up. Until you do, they're going to keep repeating themselves, playing out in your leadership, your

---

[44] (Apollo, n.d.)

relationships, and every tough conversation you have at work.

Your suitcase is yours, and everyone else's suitcase is theirs. You don't need to unpack other people's bags, and you certainly don't need to diagnose what is in them. Especially because you don't have the specialization needed to handle unpacking that suitcase (unless you are a therapist, in that case, carry on). But for the rest of us managers, that isn't our role. This chapter isn't a crash course in pop psychology so you can start labeling your employees' behaviors. It's a guide to help you recognize that everyone is carrying something, and that knowing this makes you a better, more empathetic manager.

The reality is that most people aren't out here trying to cause harm (unless they're actual sociopaths, in which case... different conversation). But people's trauma responses can cause harm anyways. We all react in ways that we don't always intend, sometimes lashing out, shutting down, or misinterpreting situations because of past wounds. The difference between an aware manager and an unaware one is the ability to recognize these dynamics without making them personal.

So no, you're not here to fix anyone. You're not here to therapize your team. But the more you understand about yourself and about human nature, the better you can show up.

Applying Trauma-Informed Management in the Workplace

Trauma-informed management isn't about walking on eggshells or lowering expectations. The goal is to recognize that *people* should always come before *process*. It's understanding that when someone has experienced trauma, recently or not, their brain isn't prioritizing creativity, productivity, or workplace synergy. It's prioritizing survival. If the brain is in survival mode, everything else, such as problem-solving, communication, and emotional regulation, takes a backseat.

For yourself, this means recognizing when you are running on stress fumes. If you've been through something difficult recently, your work will feel harder. Your patience will be thinner. Your creativity will be sluggish because your brain is too busy scanning for threats, whether real or imagined. For others, trauma and anxiety often show up in more subtle ways. They might be extra jittery, or might see an increase in mistakes, or say those casual throwaway comments like "I've been having a hard time sleeping" or "I keep waking up in the middle of the night." Those are indicators that someone's nervous system is in overdrive. That's when a simple check-in can make all the difference.

Instead of ignoring it or assuming they'll "get over it," say something like, *"I've noticed you seem a bit anxious lately. How can I best support you?"*

Work itself can be a major trigger, especially during seasons of big change. When an organization is restructuring, leadership is shifting, or expectations are evolving, it can stir up anxiety in even the most stable employees. And if that work stress is happening alongside personal upheaval? That's a perfect recipe for someone to enter survival mode, even if they don't realize it.

The best thing you can do as a leader is call it out. Not in an accusatory way, but by naming the feeling and showing them you care. Too many adults simply don't know how to label what they are experiencing (by no fault of their own—past generations didn't exactly prioritize talking about feelings). Instead, they feel off, but they can't pinpoint why. When a manager acknowledges it with something as simple as, *"This seems like a stressful time for you. I just want you to know I see it, and I'm here to support you,"* it can be a game-changer. Even if you're slightly off in your assessment, they'll correct you, and that conversation can be the first step toward them feeling seen, rather than isolated.

When we accept that trauma is part of the human experience, we level up as leaders. We stop assuming that every curt email or awkward interaction is a personal attack. We recognize that behavior—especially the kind that makes you want to bang your head against a desk—always has an origin story. Maybe the person snapping in meetings doesn't even realize they are channeling the ghost of every micromanaging boss they ever had. Maybe the employee avoiding feedback like it's the plague grew up in a house where criticism was never constructive, only crushing. The point is: People don't just wake up and decide to be difficult. Something is fueling that behavior, whether they are aware of it or not. As a leader, your job isn't to diagnose it, but to navigate it with awareness and keep the team moving forward.

That said, grace doesn't mean ignoring bad behavior. If someone is being aggressive, judgmental, or disruptive, you still need to address it. But how you address it matters. The goal isn't to shame them. It's to hold them accountable while also offering support. Instead of saying, *"You can't talk to people that way."* try:

> *"I need you to correct that and apologize. That wasn't okay. But I also want you to know that I care about you, and I don't think that reaction reflects your true character. I hope you'll take some time to reflect on what's going on. How can I support you? Do you need time off? A schedule adjustment? A lighter workload? What needs to change so that when you're here, you can show up in a way that aligns with our company's values?"*

This approach does two things. It enforces accountability while also reinforcing that you see them as a person, not just as an employee. When people feel both seen and supported, they are far more likely to take ownership of their actions and fully engage with their work.

What's in Your Toolbox?

Understanding trauma is one thing. Knowing what to do with that knowledge is another. A trauma-informed manager does not only recognize that people carry emotional suitcases, they take steps to support their team in a way that prioritizes both well-being and accountability. That doesn't mean playing therapist, and it doesn't mean lowering expectations. It means knowing what resources exist and making sure people can access them when they need support. You do not have to have all the answers, but you do need to know where to point people when they are struggling.

If your company offers access to counseling, use it. Make a point to know what's available through employee wellness programs, insurance plans, and workplace benefits. Larger organizations often bake these resources into their infrastructure, but they are useless if no one knows about them. As a manager, it's part of your job to know what is in your company's support toolkit so that when an employee is struggling, you don't have to scramble because you already have options in your back pocket.

Some workplaces even have on-site counselors. If someone is having a rough moment, your role isn't to play therapist. It's to get them to the right resource. A simple, *"I'm here to support you, but I'm not trained for this. Let's walk together to the support office,"* can be exactly what someone needs to hear. And if there's no on-site counselor? Start the process for them. Get an email chain going with the employee and the wellness coordinator. Be the bridge, not the solution.

Flexibility is another key tool. If an employee needs to see a therapist during work hours, let them. It's far better to accommodate someone proactively than to watch them burn out and spiral later. In my own role, I've even helped employees navigate their insurance plans, because let's be honest, healthcare systems are confusing on purpose. Talking to a doctor shouldn't feel like trying to solve a puzzle with missing pieces, yet for many people, it does. Sometimes, just normalizing the process and reminding people that mental health care is just as valid as physical health care makes a world of difference. If someone shares symptoms of anxiety or depression, gently guiding them to speak with a doctor could help them get a diagnosis that improves their day-to-day life.

I've even made a point to share my own journey with mental health to help normalize the conversation. I've talked about the time I spoke to my doctor about the anxiety I was feeling and how I started taking an SSRI. (Which, by the way, plenty of people take.) After a while, I thought I didn't need it anymore, then COVID hit, and suddenly, I needed it again. So, I got back on it, because my brain needed that extra support to feel safe and grounded. If someone on my team is struggling with anxiety, I share that story. Not because they need to do what I did, but because they need to know they have nothing to be ashamed of. Sometimes, the best support you can offer is simply making sure they know they're not alone.

Do Your Own Work First

The truth about trauma-informed leadership is that you are not responsible for fixing anyone. You're responsible for taking care of yourself and doing the work to understand your own patterns.

The hard part is a lot of people won't do this work. They will ignore their triggers, refuse to adapt, and eventually burn out or get pushed out. They won't deal with the stuff holding them back. But unprocessed trauma and unchecked anxiety don't disappear just because we pretend they're not there. They linger in the background, shaping decisions, creating friction, and quietly stalling growth. And while anxiety once helped our ancestors avoid actual predators, most of us are not being hunted. Still, our nervous systems haven't received the memo, so we react to emails, deadlines, and performance reviews like they're life-or-death situations.

That's why the most important work you can do as a leader is not solving other people's problems. It is knowing yourself. What is in *your* suitcase? What is shaping your reactions and influencing the way you lead?

People don't need a savior; they need an example. The best way to help others grow is to show them what growth actually looks like. If you are going to lead, you have to do your own work first. That is the job. And the more you commit to it, the better leader, and human, you will become.

Chapter 8:
Vulnerability Is the Root of
Human-Centered Management

Human-centered management is not about holding hands and singing *Kumbaya* in the breakroom—unless your team is into that, no judgment if so. It's about prioritizing your people first. Many leaders think doing this comes at the expense of business goals, but in truth it doesn't. In fact, it's the path to achieving them.

New managers often fall into the key performance indicator (KPI) trap. They think if they just push hard by enforcing deadlines, tracking metrics, holding people "accountable" (which is usually code for micromanaging), then results will magically follow. Spoiler alert! They won't. Because people aren't machines. When you prioritize the numbers over the humans producing them, your team starts checking out. That's how you get burnout, disengagement, and a whole lot of "working" that looks suspiciously like scrolling LinkedIn for better jobs.

Think of your team like a garden. You can't just stomp into the greenhouse, yell at the tomatoes to ripen faster, and expect a miracle. You have to tend to them. You have to give them water, sunlight, and fertilizer. If you want people to grow, you have to invest in them, and that means showing up in ways that matter.

It starts with consistent, quality time. I don't need to know every detail of someone's personal life, but I do need to care about them as a person before I focus on them as an

Kate Vawter

employee. That means scheduling regular check-ins, including team meetings at least twice a month, ideally weekly, and one on ones with each direct report. A new employee should have these weekly, no exceptions. For seasoned employees, once or twice a month is fine, and they can decide if scaling down makes sense. These meetings are a high priority, and they shouldn't only be focused on performance. They should be focused on building trust. Every conversation is a chance to lay another brick in the foundation of that relationship, which pays dividends when challenges arise.

When you don't prioritize building relationships based on trust, especially as a leader, you create a culture of uncertainty, hesitation, and disengagement. Without trust, people hold back, communication suffers, and teams become transactional rather than collaborative. Instead of innovation, you get fear. Instead of accountability, you get avoidance. And instead of a thriving, connected workplace, you end up with a group of individuals trying to get through the day without stepping on a landmine.

I once worked at a company where a new VP came in hot. He offered no real introductions and no real effort to get to know us. Instead, he threw us into brainstorming sessions where he sat silently, watching, judging, seemingly scheming how to pit us against each other. It felt less like collaboration and more like we were being judged on an invisible scorecard. Then one day—*poof!*—two people were gone. No warning. No explanation. Just…vanished.

You can bet none of us felt safe after that. If two people could disappear without a word, what did that mean for the rest of us? Every meeting after that carried an underlying tension. Were we next? Should we speak up, or would that put a target on our backs? It was clear that trust wasn't a priority, transparency wasn't a given, and job security was a guessing game. Instead of fostering collaboration, the VP had created an environment where we second-guessed every decision. When people don't feel secure, they don't take risks, they don't innovate, and they certainly don't give their best work.

This is the opposite of human-centered management. Leadership isn't about storming in, making snap judgments, and pulling the trigger before you even understand the team you're leading. It's about relationships first and decisions second. When people feel valued, they work harder, stay longer, and actually care about the work they're doing. That's how you hit your business goals without running your team into the ground.

Now, none of this means you have to be a perfect manager. In fact, aiming for perfection is one of the fastest ways to fail. You're not some omniscient leadership guru with all the right answers—no one is. You are a human leading other humans, all of whom have their own quirks, challenges, and, let's-be-honest, occasional bad days where even they wouldn't want to work with themselves.

The truth is relationships aren't built on perfection. They are built on consistency, trust, and the willingness to show up, even when things get messy. And they *will* get messy. People will make mistakes (or human errors as I like to call them), and so will you. The real test of leadership isn't about getting everything right; it's about how you handle it when you don't. That is where human-centered leadership really comes into play.

Expect Imperfection

If there's one universal truth about management, it's that no one has it all figured out. Not you. Not your employees. Not even that executive who somehow gets invited to every leadership panel but hasn't done a single meaningful thing since 2014. Yet, for some reason, the default management style tends to expect perfection, both from ourselves and those around us.

We pile the pressure on thick. We convince ourselves that to be a *good* manager, we have to be excellent in every area of leadership all the time. We must have the right words, the right tone, and the right responses. We must never fumble or miss a beat. And when we inevitably do? Cue the shame, the guilt, and the all-too-familiar three am spiral where we ask ourselves, "Did I handle that right? Am I the worst boss ever? Should I quit and stock grocery shelves instead?"

I'm not the first to say perfection is a myth, and I certainly won't be the last. But I'll say it here because for you to be a human-centered leader, you have to truly understand that this expectation is not only unrealistic, but it actively works against you. You're managing *humans*, not spreadsheets. And humans? We are a messy, unpredictable bunch. Each of us carries a lifetime of experiences, some good, some bad, some we'd rather forget—queue the trauma suitcase we discussed in the previous chapter.

As a manager, you're going to have employees who have packed light, people who breeze through challenges without breaking a sweat. You're also going to have employees who are carrying so much in their suitcase that a single, seemingly small workplace stressor can send them into full-blown survival mode. Not because they're dramatic. Not because they're difficult. But because that one moment is the latest in a long line of experiences that have told them *you are not safe here.*

I once worked with a client who was thrilled to land a new job at a company they had loved since childhood, a place tied to some of their happiest memories. And for them, it was more than a paycheck. They had grown up in the cycle of poverty, and this workplace was a chance to build a stable future.

Yet, they only lasted two weeks. Why? Because one coworker bullied them out of the door. They whispered in their ear, made snide comments about their relationships, and generally made them feel unsafe. It wasn't overt bullying, just enough quiet manipulation to make every workday feel like walking through a minefield.

Someone else who has less trauma in their suitcase might have told that coworker to shove it and move on. But for this employee, it was too much. The stress, the anxiety, the years of trauma in their suitcase they had brought from their previous workplace and from their life all weighed heavily on them. So, they quit. And their manager was left wondering what happened.

One of the hardest lessons in management is realizing that people don't always behave in ways that make sense to you because their suitcase isn't packed like yours.

A common question almost every manager has asked a direct report is, "Why did you do that?" It slips out easily, especially when we're confused, frustrated, or just trying to make sense of someone's actions. But intention isn't the same as impact. We might ask this question with truly open curiosity and no judgement. But for someone with a heavy suitcase filled with past trauma, this question can feel like an interrogation because their brain has already slammed the panic button before they even have a chance to process your words.

What they *hear* isn't always what you *say*. You ask, *Why did you do that?* They hear, *You screwed up. Defend yourself.* You say, *I need to talk to you later.* They hear, *You're in trouble.*

Remember when we discussed that emotions are the brain's way of predicting what's happening, even if it isn't what's actually happening? When someone has a history of negative or high-stress experiences, whether from childhood, past relationships, or toxic workplaces, their brain wires itself for protection. This means their nervous system doesn't wait to assess the intent behind a question like, "Why did you do that?" It detects a threat and flips into fight, flight, freeze, or fawn mode.

For some employees, that means defensiveness. They push back, over-explain, or shut down. Others may try to appease, telling you what they think you want to hear rather than what's true. And then there are those who simply go blank. Not because they don't care, but because their brain is too busy rerouting power to survival mode to formulate a coherent response.

This isn't dramatics. This is science. For some people, their amygdala doesn't know the difference between a lion chasing them and a boss asking, "Why did you do that?" If someone has a history of being punished, shamed, or blindsided in response to that kind of question, their brain takes a shortcut and tells their body, "Last time this happened, it didn't end well. Sound the alarm." Then what started as a simple question turns into a full-blown stress response.

Being a human-centered manager isn't about sugarcoating or coddling. But it does require you to recognize how different people process interactions and adjust accordingly. If someone's brain is too busy defending itself from an imagined threat, they aren't hearing you. Instead, they are hearing every bad experience that question has ever led to in their past.

When you manage with a human-centered approach, you start to recognize these patterns. You start to see that your words, no matter how well-intentioned, don't always land the way you expect them to. Make adjustments. If you want better communication (and fewer employees spiraling into existential dread over a casual Slack message), you need to be intentional with your language.

Instead of: *"Why did you do that?"*
Try: *"Help me understand how you got there."*
This shifts the focus from blame to curiosity. It signals that you want insight, not excuses.

Instead of: *"We need to talk."*
Try: *"Hey, could I grab ten minutes with you today to go over [specific topic] so I can be prepared for [insert meeting]?"*

This removes the ambiguity and gives context, so they don't spend hours bracing for bad news.

Instead of: *"Did you get that thing done yet?"*
Try: *"Hey, random check-in—how are you doing?"*
This keeps the conversation open and human instead of making them feel like a task-completing robot.

When it comes to performance reviews? Set the tone from the start. Instead of letting someone sweat for days wondering if they're about to be blindsided, try: *"I'm excited to go over everything you've accomplished this year."* Because—nine times out of ten—that's the truth. Their work *should* be celebrated.

Yesterday, I was in a meeting with a business owner and a manager. We were discussing job duties, talking about people who weren't in the room, and sorting through decisions we needed to make for the betterment of the business. Then, we pivoted and called in an employee. This person walked into a room where three people in positions of power had been talking privately for an hour.

The tension was immediate. They looked like a deer in the headlights. So, the first thing I said was, *"You're not fired. You're not in trouble."* Because I know how that moment feels. I know that for someone with a heavy suitcase, being unexpectedly called into a meeting with multiple higher-ups can be terrifying. It can bring up past experiences like getting in trouble at school, being called out by a parent, being blindsided by a previous boss.

When you manage with a human-centered approach, you anticipate these moments. You recognize that what you say and what someone hears aren't always the same thing. And you adjust accordingly.

Remember, you are managing people, not just their work, but their experiences, their histories, and their fears. You're not responsible for fixing what they've been through. But you are responsible for leading with awareness and meeting them with empathy.

Relationships Require Hats and Vulnerability

Relationships, whether personal or professional, are rarely one-dimensional. We don't show up as just one thing to the people in our lives. Instead, we cycle through different roles, sometimes in the span of a single day.

In any given workplace, you might wear the mentor hat, guiding an employee through a tricky challenge. An hour later, you're in supervisor mode, holding someone accountable for missing a deadline. Later that afternoon, you're a coach, offering encouragement to someone struggling with confidence. And maybe, just maybe, over lunch, you slide into friend territory, laughing about the absurdity of an all-staff email that somehow went completely off the rails.

Each of these roles comes with different expectations. Different levels of authority. Different ways of engaging. Most importantly, different levels of vulnerability. Because relationships at their core are built on trust, and trust is built through vulnerability.

Now, not all relationships start with deep trust and openness. In fact, very few do. Trust is a slow build, something that grows over time, piece by piece. Let's say you have a brand-new employee. You're not expecting them to waltz in on day one and start sharing their childhood traumas over a cup of coffee. Nor are you, as their manager, expected to give them a deep dive into your personal life right off the bat. That's not how trust works.

In the early stages of any relationship, especially professional ones, vulnerability is like a dimmer switch, not an on/off button. You don't start at full brightness. You start with a low, manageable glow. Then as positive interactions build and people show they can be trusted, the light gradually grows brighter.

I always recommend letting time build your trust. Forced vulnerability, the kind we've all experienced when companies trot out the "we're all family here" speech to encourage emotional oversharing, can be dangerous. Being completely open with someone we barely know puts us at risk. If they haven't earned our trust, there's always the chance they could use what we share against us. And in a work environment? That risk is even higher.

Yet, for something so essential, vulnerability is wildly misunderstood. Some people hear the word vulnerability and immediately think of *weakness*. Especially in American work culture, where toughness is prized, and "keeping it professional" is often code for "don't show emotion." Others see vulnerability as an all-or-nothing deal—either you're an open book, spilling your deepest thoughts to everyone who asks, or you keep everything locked down, never letting anyone see behind the curtain. Both of those perspectives are nonsense.

Vulnerability isn't weakness; it's the foundation of every meaningful relationship you'll ever have. And vulnerability happens in layers. Some levels are easier, almost automatic. Others take time and careful trust-building to reach. I believe there are five levels of vulnerability. These levels help us understand how we engage in relationships, both at work and beyond. Let's break them down.

Vulnerability Level 1: Common Experiences

This is the entry-level vulnerability and includes sharing things that are universal. We all need to eat, sleep, wear clothes, and function as humans in the world. Talking about these things is effortless because they don't reveal much about who we are beyond the basic fact that we exist.

It's the difference between saying, "Ugh, I didn't sleep well last night" versus "I didn't sleep well last night because I was spiraling about that email I sent at three pm, and now I think my boss secretly hates me." One is a fact of life, the other starts inching into deeper emotional territory.

At work, this level of vulnerability is everywhere. Casual kitchen talk about the weather, mentioning what you had for dinner, grumbling about needing coffee to function—all of it falls into the safe to share category. Nobody's going to take "I went grocery shopping" and use it as ammunition in a performance review. But move up a level, and things start to get a little more personal.

Vulnerability Level 2: Personal Preferences

Here's where we step beyond just existing and start sharing who we are. It's moving from telling someone you went grocery shopping to explaining that you grocery shop at Trader Joe's because you appreciate their price point and the small footprint of the store. Or that you refuse to drink office coffee because you're a die-hard espresso person and can't handle the watered-down swill that comes out of the communal machine.

At this level, we're sharing small insights into our identity including our tastes, our opinions, and the little things that make us who we are. There's still very little risk here, but it's more revealing than level one.

In a work setting, this might be the point where you start to see personalities emerge. One coworker always brings their lunch from home because they love meal prepping. Another swears by a particular productivity app and recommends it to everyone. These preferences tell us a little more about a person, but they don't expose anything particularly vulnerable. It's still surface level.

Vulnerability Level 3: Personal Experiences

Now we're entering real sharing territory. It's not just that you went grocery shopping—it's that while you were there, you ran into an old friend who recommended a new product, so you tried it, and it turned out to be amazing. This is where we start offering up our stories.

At work, this level of vulnerability looks like sharing an anecdote about a past job, talking about a challenge you overcame, or mentioning a meaningful experience that shaped how you think. It's the kind of sharing that builds relationships, because it gives people insight into how we move through the world.

But it's still pretty safe. You're offering up a piece of your life, but it's only a *piece*. The information shared isn't deeply personal or risky. You're still in comfortable territory.

Vulnerability Level 4: Personal Thoughts

This is where vulnerability really starts to kick in. You move from telling a story about a product you tried, to explaining why you like that product and what it does for you.

This might not sound like a big jump, but it is. At this level, we're no longer just sharing what happened, we're sharing what we think about it. Thoughts, unlike experiences, open us up to disagreement, judgment, and potential *rejection*.

At work, this is where people start to voice opinions that might not be universally agreed upon. "I actually think this process isn't working and we should try something different." That's vulnerability. You're putting yourself out there with an idea, knowing someone might disagree.

This is also where self-doubt can creep in. At this level, rejection stings a little more. It's one thing for someone to brush off your story about trying a new product. It's another for them to dismiss your actual opinion about it.

Vulnerability Level 5: Personal Growth

This is the deep stuff. Instead of telling someone you like a specific hand lotion, it's telling them that you have set a goal to take better care of your body this year, and part of that goal is paying more attention to your skin, which is why you're making a point to use this hand lotion.

At this level, you're sharing why what you are doing matters to you. You're exposing a part of yourself that, if the wrong person hears it, could be used against you. They might judge you with snide comments like "Oh great, it's the weird hand lotion lady." Or they might disagree with you and say, "If you want to take care of your skin, you should focus on facial cleansers instead."

This is the level where sharing is the most risky. This is where we open up about our aspirations, our struggles, and our personal journeys. At work, this might be admitting, "I've been working on speaking up more in meetings because I know I tend to hold back." Or "I'm really trying to be a better listener with my team, and it's something I have to consciously work on."

This level of vulnerability isn't something we share with just anyone. It requires real trust, because the wrong reaction can be *crushing*. That's why, in most cases, we save it for the people we've built a history with. But trust doesn't always follow a predictable path. In fact, some of the deepest, most honest conversations happen with people we'll never see again. Have you ever spilled your guts to a stranger on a plane or told your most personal thoughts to an Uber driver, knowing you'll never cross paths again? That's because when there's no ongoing relationship, there is minimal risk. They can't use what we've shared against us, so the usual hesitation disappears.

In the workplace, where relationships are ongoing, we are more careful. And that's okay. The key is recognizing that vulnerability is a spectrum. With a brand-new coworker, you might stay at levels one or two. With someone you've worked with for years, you might be at level five. Both are valid. Here's a helpful graphic to use when considering what level of vulnerability is appropriate.

The Vulnerability Spectrum in Action

Knowing the levels is one thing, but using them in real life is another. So, what does it look like to navigate vulnerability at work? Let's say you're meeting a new team member for the first time. You keep it light and say something like, "Hey, nice to meet you! How's your day going?" This is easy, universal, zero-risk, and is level one vulnerability.

After a few chats, you might show a bit more personality and say something like, "I love working from coffee shops. There's this one downtown I really like."

This is level two vulnerability. It's still safe, but a little more personal.

Now fast-forward a few months. You've collaborated, built trust, seen how each other works. That's when you might share more of yourself and say, "Last weekend, I went to this concert and ran into an old friend, it was such a full-circle moment." This is level three vulnerability and isn't oversharing while offering a safe way to connect.

Then, a big project challenge comes up, and you've got a different take from them on how to approach it. You might say something like, "I think we should handle this another way. Here's why." That's level four vulnerability. You're sharing ideas knowing there is a risk of disagreement.

Eventually, if the relationship continues to grow, you might feel safe enough to say, "I've been struggling with imposter syndrome lately. I'm working on it." That's level five trust. That's someone who knows they won't be judged for being real.

You don't start with this level of openness; it's built over time. Just like you wouldn't walk into a first date and launch into your deepest insecurities, professional relationships need space to evolve. When someone seems quiet, hesitant, or closed off, it's not necessarily disengagement. It might mean they're still building trust with you. Your role as a human-centered leader isn't to force vulnerability—it's to create the kind of environment where it feels safe to show up fully, one level at a time.

The goal isn't to get everyone to level five. The goal is to respect where people are, recognize the cues, and meet them there with curiosity, not pressure.

The Trust Marble Jar

Brené Brown told a story in one of Opera's Super Soul Sessions about her daughter, Ellen, who came home from school one day completely devastated.[45] She had shared a personal secret with her best friend, and that secret was something she already felt a little ashamed about. Sadly, that friend turned around and told *everyone*. As Ellen sat in tears, struggling to understand what had just happened, Brené found herself trying to explain trust to a seven-year-old. Like any good teacher, she reached for an analogy.

Ellen's classroom had a marble jar. When the class behaved well, the teacher would add marbles to the jar. When they didn't, marbles came out. If the class filled the jar to a certain level, they'd earn a reward such as a pizza party or extra recess.

Brené explained to Ellen that trust works the same way. Every relationship we have is its own marble jar. In the beginning, the jar is empty. As people show us they are trustworthy through consistency, kindness, and respect, they add marbles to our trust jar. But when trust is broken, marbles come out.

The idea is simple but powerful. It also applies in the workplace.

In professional relationships, trust isn't something that's automatically granted. It's built, one small moment at a time. Every interaction, whether it's a conversation in the break room, an email exchange, or how you handle conflict, adds or removes marbles from the jar. But unlike Ellen's classroom, where everyone was working toward the

---

[45] (Brown, n.d.)

same goal (a pizza party), in the workplace, each person has their own independent trust jar with every other person they interact with.

When a new employee walks into the company on their first day, their trust jars with every coworker, manager, and leader are empty. Maybe they come in assuming goodwill, ready to start adding marbles the moment someone shows kindness. Or maybe they enter cautiously, waiting to see if the environment is truly safe before they start placing their trust in anyone. Some people (especially those of us with past experiences that have taught us to be wary) might need time to let their marble jar even open, let alone start filling.

Remember, this goes both ways. Employees don't automatically trust their managers just because they have a title. Managers need to earn those marbles, just like employees do.

A lot of leaders make the mistake of assuming they start with a full jar and believe that trust comes with authority. But that's not how human nature works. People trust *actions*, not titles. They trust behavior over time, not a job description. You can have a brand-new manager walk into a team of seasoned professionals, and their jars are just as empty as the new employee's jar. The only way to fill them is through consistency, respect, and follow-through.

One of the fastest ways to build trust in a new relationship is through shared experiences and small moments of connection. A simple, "How was your weekend?" can be the first step. When we find common ground, we instinctively start placing marbles in the jar. Maybe it's discovering that you and a coworker both love hiking. Maybe it's realizing that someone else also struggles with imposter syndrome. These little moments don't seem like much, but they add up.

When I run workshops with people I haven't worked with before, I always start by sharing something small about myself, something that falls into level one or two of vulnerability. I put up pictures of me with my dog, me hiking, maybe even a picture of me and a friend out on the town. Then I'll ask questions like, "Do we have any dog owners here?" or "Does anyone like hiking?" When I share and someone relates, it creates a thread of connection between us. That connection makes people more engaged, more curious, and more likely to go deeper. Because trust builds fastest when you go first.

Then, once trust is built, it needs to be maintained. That's where things get trickier, because just as marbles can be added, they can also be taken out.

One of the most common ways trust erodes in the workplace is through broken commitments. If I miss a deadline, that's a marble out of my trust jar with my manager. If I don't communicate why, that's another one gone. However, if I meet with my boss, explain what happened, and outline how I'll prevent it from happening again, that might put a marble back in. Trust doesn't require perfection, but it does require accountability.

Another surefire way to drain marbles? Passive-aggressive communication. *Per my last email. Just circling back. Let me know if I misunderstood.* These phrases might seem harmless, but with the wrong tone, they basically say, "I don't trust you," without actually using those words.

Every time a passive-aggressive email lands in someone's inbox, marbles fly out of the jar.

But the biggest marble dump of all? Gossip. If I tell a coworker that I'm struggling with something, and later I hear from a different person, "Hey, I heard you were having a rough day," that's an immediate marble dump for me. Because now I know my words weren't safe. Trust requires safety. Nothing erodes safety faster than realizing your private words weren't kept private. Whether it's a personal struggle, a workplace frustration, or even a minor complaint, when information spreads without consent, trust disappears. Once a jar is dumped this way, filling it back up is a long, slow process. Here are a few trust builders and breakers to keep in mind:

Trust Builders	Trust Breakers
• Following through on commitments • Owning mistakes and making them right • Giving credit where it's due • Listening without interrupting • Being consistent and reliable • Offering help without being asked • Providing clear and timely communication • Admitting when you don't know something • Being transparent about decisions • Holding yourself accountable • Speaking up respectfully when there's a concern • Recognizing and appreciating others • Checking in with others, especially during stressful times • Clarifying expectations early and often • Giving space for others' ideas and input • Keeping your emotions in check under pressure • Showing up prepared and on time	• Missing deadlines • Blaming others • Taking credit for someone else's work • Gossiping about coworkers • Withholding important information • Playing favorites or showing bias • Avoiding difficult conversations • Dismissing others' ideas or concerns • Showing up late or unprepared • Making decisions behind closed doors • Sharing confidential info without consent • Reacting emotionally instead of responding professionally • Ignoring feedback or defensiveness when it's given • Being inconsistent with expectations or rules • Talking over or interrupting others • Not acknowledging others' contributions • Invalidating people's experiences or emotions • Acting one way with staff and another with leadership

Leadership Is a Love Language

The goal of human-centered management isn't just to have a few marbles in the trust jar or scale the five levels of vulnerability. It's to create strong relationships and open communication so the team knows they can rely on each other. When we talk about building trust in human-centered management, we're really talking about showing up in four of the five love languages. Don't worry about physical, you don't have to go hugging your employees or holding their hands (please don't). But you do have to be intentional about how you support them. Let's take a closer look at how these love languages can help build trust in the workplace.

Quality Time

This happens in one-on-one meetings, where you give employees your full attention. No checking emails, no half-listening while thinking about your next task, but really being present. The more consistently you offer these conversations, the more trust builds.

Words of Affirmation

Recognizing effort. Acknowledging growth. Giving credit where it's due. People don't only want to hear feedback when they mess up, they want to know when they're doing something well. Even a simple, "Hey, I noticed how you handled that tough conversation. You did a great job," can add marbles to the jar.

Acts of Service

A real leader doesn't simply point to the goal. They walk alongside the team to help get them there. Sometimes, trust is built by stepping in and helping when it's needed.

Maybe it's staying late to assist on a big project. Maybe it's clearing roadblocks so someone can do their job better. These small actions show your team that you don't just expect things from them, you're also willing to give.

Gifts (or Appropriate Compensation/Benefits/Bonuses)

This one doesn't mean buying Starbucks gift cards for everyone (though, hey, if that's your style, go for it). In a work setting, this often looks like ensuring employees are fairly compensated, advocating for their professional growth, and giving recognition in meaningful ways. If the team hits a major milestone, celebrate it. If someone's going above and beyond, acknowledge it with something tangible.

Touch, of course, is the one love language that doesn't belong in the workplace. But that's fine. There are more than enough ways to build trust without physical gestures.

Beyond these actions, real trust is also built in the small moments. It's in listening without jumping to fix. It's in validating someone's experience instead of brushing it off. It's in being honest when you don't know the answer instead of pretending you have it all figured out. And, just as importantly, it's in knowing when and how to share your own vulnerabilities.

When we lead with trust, vulnerability, and emotional intelligence, we create the conditions for real connection. It's that connection that allows vulnerability to take root. As leaders, we're constantly shifting roles to meet the needs of the people we manage. Some days, you're the mentor. Other days, you're the coach, the supervisor, the sounding board, or the person who gently suggests everyone take a breath and maybe get a snack. Each role asks for a different version of you, and knowing when to switch hats is a skill worth learning. Next, we'll break down the different hats you'll wear as a manager and what each one requires.

Chapter 9:
Wearing the Mentor Hat

Up to this point, we have laid the emotional foundation of human-centered leadership. We've explored the internal and external struggles that come with stepping into management, unpacked the discomfort of growth, and learned how emotional regulation shapes how you lead. We've analyzed what motivates people from the inside out, how values anchor your decisions, how trauma impacts behavior, and why vulnerability is the root of real trust.

Now, it's time to take everything you've learned and put it into motion.

No matter how grounded, present, or trustworthy you are, the job still requires you to *do stuff.* As managers, we are expected to guide performance, navigate conflict, support growth, and make hard decisions. To do that well, we need to step into a variety of roles. This is where you'll need to wear a few different hats.

Each of these hats represents a distinct function of your role as a manager. They require different tools, different energy, and a different version of you. But you will use everything you've learned so far in each of them. Some days, you'll switch between all five before lunch. Other days, you'll wear one so heavily it will feel like it's been superglued to your skull.

Here are the five core hats you'll need to know. Keep in mind: there may be more hats for you. These aren't the only hats out there. But as I've worked with my clients and have been in my own leadership positions, they are the five hats that are most commonly used.

- **The Mentor:** Help people grow through guidance.
- **The Coach**: Ask powerful questions and challenge growth edges.
- **The Supervisor**: Set clear expectations, offer feedback, and hold others accountable.
- **The Friend**: Build connection and camaraderie while maintaining healthy boundaries.
- **The Leader**: Cast vision, make decisions, bring people together, and model what matters most.

Each hat serves a purpose and has strengths, risks, and specific moments where it's the right one to wear. But they don't work in isolation. Great managers know how to shift between them fluidly, depending on the needs of their team and the demands of the moment.

In this chapter, we'll start with the Mentor Hat because if you want a team that sticks around and levels up, you need to be more than a boss—you need to be a guide.

Mentorship Means More Than, "Hey, Do This"

It's your first week at a new job. You've been added to a meeting invite with no explanation, and five minutes before it starts, your manager swings by your desk and says, "Hey, take notes."

That's it. No guidance on what's important, no format to follow, just an expectation that you'll somehow document the entire conversation in a way that makes sense to everyone. You open a blank document and stare at the screen. Do they want bullet points? Full sentences? A summary? Should you capture who said what, or just the action items? You have no idea. By the time the meeting ends, you've got a mess of half-sentences, vague references to "that thing we talked about," and absolutely no idea what actually happened. Congratulations, you've just experienced mentoring failure in real-time.

This is what happens when managers forget to put on their mentor hat. It's the hat we need to wear when we teach the hard skills our team needs to do their jobs well. Whether it's drafting meeting notes, creating an Excel report, setting up a project timeline, or coordinating team logistics, hard skills have a clear outcome: they're either right or they're not.

Saying "Hey, do this" is not teaching. It's barely even communicating. Real mentorship requires showing, explaining, and reinforcing. It means being a resource, not just a taskmaster. Sometimes, it means knowing when to step back and let someone else on the team take the lead in teaching. A great manager doesn't have to be an expert at every skill in the room, but they do have to make sure the right knowledge is being shared.

Learning sticks when people understand both the what and the why. Instead of just teaching someone how to do a task, explain why it's done that way. Processes don't exist randomly. Sometimes, a specific workflow saves time, prevents mistakes, or fits within company standards. Other times, there's a long history behind why things are done a certain way. When employees understand the reasoning, they will hold onto the knowledge much longer.

Nobody likes struggling through a task without proper guidance. There is an easy way to do things and a hard way, and part of your role as a mentor is to make sure your employees don't take the hard way if they don't have to. Shift your mindset from "I need this task done" to "I need this person to feel confident doing this task."

Step One in Every New Work Relationship

When a new member joins your team, they are bright-eyed, slightly nervous, and trying to decode the office coffee situation without looking like a lost puppy. Meanwhile, you are eager to get them up to speed, and you're already thinking about all the things they need to learn. But learning requires trust, and they don't trust you yet. You haven't earned that. Right now, you're just the person who signs their checks and decides whether or not they get in trouble for using too many exclamation points in their email.

So where do you start? With the mentor hat.

The challenge is that teaching hard skills requires giving feedback. Giving feedback means telling people that some part of their work isn't quite right. There's an art to this because the last thing you want to do is shake their confidence before they've even started and drain the few marbles that are already in the trust jar. Too often, managers default to pointing out everything that's wrong, assuming they're being helpful. But your employee likely already knows what they messed up. They feel it. They see it. So, when you swoop in and focus only on their mistakes, you're not teaching, you're reinforcing their own self-doubt.

Before diving into what needs fixing, start with what's working. When someone has put effort into a task, acknowledge that first. "This part is perfect, and this is exactly what we need," or you might say, "You nailed this section. It's clear, well-organized, and exactly the format we want." A simple shift in approach can completely change how feedback is received. Instead of feeling like they've failed, they will understand what they should keep doing while staying open to improving the parts that need work.

One way to keep feedback balanced and productive is by using the sandwich method (an old method I use consistently): starting with a positive, addressing the area that needs improvement, and ending with another positive. Now, the goal here isn't to sugarcoat the truth. Instead, it's about making sure the conversation stays constructive rather than feeling like an attack. Instead of leading with, *"This isn't what we need,"* try something like, *"I really like how you structured this. It's clear and professional."* Then, ease into the necessary critique and say, *"One area we can improve is the tone. It needs to be a little more formal to match our executive communication style."* Finally, reinforce their effort. *"Overall, this is a strong start, and I really appreciate the work you put into it."*

It might seem small, but this approach makes a big difference. Instead of leaving the conversation feeling defeated, your employee walks away with clear direction, confidence in what they did well, and motivation to improve. It also keeps you, as the mentor, accountable for maintaining a respectful and supportive environment rather than defaulting to frustration when things aren't perfect.

Even if the final product isn't where it needs to be, acknowledging the time and energy someone put into their work builds trust. When an employee knows their effort is valued, they're more likely to stay motivated and engaged in the learning process. A simple comment like, "I can tell you put a lot of time into this, and I really appreciate that," goes a long way to help others feel safe learning and refining their skills rather than fearing that every misstep will be picked apart.

Finally, remember to invite your team members into the process. Once they have learned a new task, you can challenge them to come to your next check-in with three things they want to improve or learn next. When employees have a say in their own learning, they develop the ability to self-assess, which is a skill that will serve them—and you—far beyond this one task.

Patience, Grasshopper

If you're a fast-moving, get-shit-done kind of person—congratulations!—you're probably in management. High-speed decision-makers and efficiency-driven doers tend to climb the ranks quickly. While that's great for productivity, it can be less great when it comes to mentoring because not everyone operates at your speed.

For those of us who naturally move fast, it can be frustrating when a team member doesn't seem to "get it" as quickly as we did. We explain something once, assume it's locked in, and then get confused (or mildly enraged) when it's not. But the truth is most people are not naturally fast learners. The fact that you can knock out a task in five minutes doesn't mean your team members should be able to do the same. Speed is not the same thing as competence.

Learning curves exist, and they vary wildly. Some people need to see a process multiple times before they feel comfortable. Others need to do it themselves before it clicks. Now, there are the exceptions for the ones who struggle beyond what's expected, and that's a different conversation. But for the majority of employees, learning a role isn't a one-week boot camp; it's a long game.

The best employees aren't necessarily the ones who master things quickly. They are the ones who take the time to learn them well. A solid, confident, self-sufficient employee typically needs about twelve months to truly settle into their role because every job has nuances, exceptions, and seasonal shifts that take time to understand. The first time they encounter a weird scenario or an outlier situation, they won't know how to handle it. The second time, they'll recognize it but still need guidance. By the third or fourth time, they've hopefully got it locked in.

As a mentor, your job is to recognize that different people process information in different ways and at different speeds. The impatient manager might see an employee struggling and think, *Why can't they just get this already?* But the manager who puts their mentor hat on takes a breath and reminds themselves that this person is still in the learning phase.

If you've explained something ten times and they still don't get it, you're the problem. I know, I know—easier to assume they're not paying attention, right? But the reality is if an employee isn't picking up a skill after repeated attempts, it's time to change your teaching approach.

162

In fact, I'd say don't wait for ten times. If a concept isn't sticking after two or three explanations, you need to switch tactics. Some people learn best by watching, so have them shadow someone who already knows the ropes. Others learn by doing, so set up smaller, lower-stakes practice runs before expecting them to handle the real thing. This could look like spot checks, guided walkthroughs, or incremental ownership of a task until they are flying solo. Personally, I prefer to teach through the scaffolding method.

The Scaffolding Method

Let me share a common scenario. As a manager, you have a project that needs to get done and a new individual on your team ready to prove themselves. So, you assign that project to them, set a deadline, and wait. Then, when the due date rolls around, the final product lands in your inbox, and…it's completely off base. Now you're scrambling to fix it at the last minute, frustrated that they "didn't get it."

This is one of the most common mentoring mistakes I see managers make. The problem isn't that your employee didn't try hard enough or didn't ask enough questions. The problem is that they were expected to deliver a polished result without direction. You essentially wanted them to read your mind, then got angry when they didn't.

This is where the scaffolding method comes in. It's a concept I borrowed from the field of education and included within the mentor hat.[46] Unlike traditional top-down teaching, scaffolding is learner-centric, meaning it's

---

[46] (Staake, 2024)

built around the way the mentee absorbs and applies new information. Instead of throwing someone into the deep end and hoping for the best, scaffolding breaks a task into meaningful, achievable steps, allowing someone to build skills gradually and with proper guidance.

Let's say you have a team member responsible for drafting memos to executives. If they've never done it before, you don't say, "Hey, write that memo and send it to me by Thursday." That's a one-way ticket to disaster. Instead, you break the process into stages, creating multiple touch points along the way.

First, have them send you an outline, a structured list of the key points they think should be included. You meet, go over it, and explain what's important, what's not, and why certain elements should be emphasized or cut. Once they've got that down, they move to the drafting stage, writing the first version based on your feedback. This first draft ends with another deadline and another check-in. This time, the conversation shifts to tone, clarity, and value. You review with them what works, what doesn't, and how to align the language with the institution's standards. They revise, submit a new version, and you meet once more for final tweaks. By the time the actual deadline for the memo arrives, they've been coached through the entire process and have a much higher chance of delivering something polished and usable on their own next time.

Now, compared to what normally happens (a vague assignment, no interim feedback, and a mad scramble the night before to fix the completely off-track memo), the scaffolding method has a much higher chance of giving someone the knowledge they need to move forward and confidently do a job well.

Yes, this approach will require time and energy from you when an employee is learning something new. The little bit of extra time you spend thoughtfully crafting a scaffolded learning model will save you loads of time over the long-run with this employee. Scaffolding ensures that people aren't crushed under the weight of an assignment they were never properly guided through. It allows them to learn in stages, not shocks, which means they improve faster and with much less frustration. Best of all? Once they've gone through the scaffolded process a few times, they won't need it anymore. They'll know what's expected, and they will produce quality work on their own without you having to rescue them at the last minute.

Stay in Your Lane (For Now)

When you put on your mentor hat, it's tempting to jump ahead. Maybe you want to be the approachable friend, or maybe you're itching to step into the supervisor role and start measuring performance. But different hats exist for a reason, and in the early days of a new hire, the mentor hat is the one that matters most.

Right now, your role is to teach, not to build deep relationships or assess long-term performance. A new employee isn't your friend, not yet. You can be friendly, sure, but expecting instant trust or emotional connection is unrealistic. At this stage, your relationship is purely transactional. They were hired to do a job, and you are here to help them learn how to do it. The foundation of your communication should be task-centric, with just enough personal connection to create a supportive learning environment. Here is a pie chart of your communication in the early days, versus five years later:

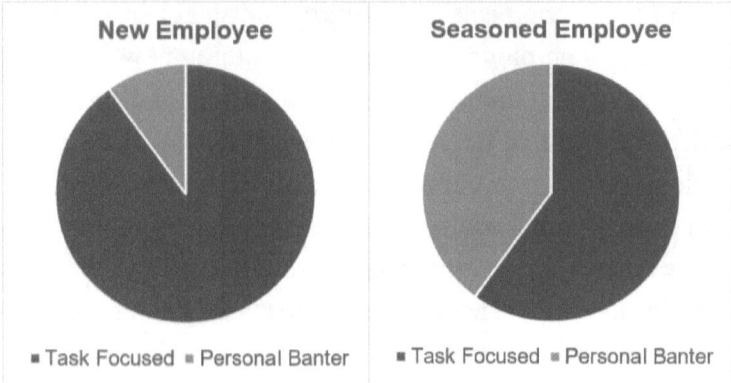

If you've worked with someone for a few years, the balance shifts. At that point, your conversations are less "Here's how to do this" and more "Hey, how was your weekend?" or "Can you believe what happened on that show last night?" The work is second nature to them, so your role leans toward coaching, fine-tuning, and the occasional venting session about that one impossible client.

But with a brand-new employee, you're their guide to surviving the wild terrain of their new role. So, save the deep heart to hearts for later and focus on making sure they don't get lost in the weeds.

Advise Them to Be a Sponge

One of the biggest mistakes new managers make is expecting perfection too soon. When you wear your mentor hat, you need to allow space for daily "mistakes." Even if (in my opinion) they aren't actually mistakes. They are moments where an employee didn't fully understand the task, outcome, or expectations. That's normal. That's learning. The mentor hat is the one that gives them room to get things wrong and figure it out with your guidance.

This is also the moment when a new employee is forming their workplace identity, and they need guardrails. One of the best pieces of advice you can give them is this:

"I want you to be a sponge for the first six months. Learn everything you can. Observe how things work. While I deeply value your opinions and ideas, you haven't put enough marbles in everybody's trust jar yet to tell the organization what it's doing wrong. So, for now, listen. Take notes. Journal about the ideas you have and the things you'd do differently. I'd love to hear them once you get the full picture and history of why we do things the way we do."

It takes about six months for a new hire to understand the full landscape of an organization. That's how long it takes to see the patterns, the exceptions, and the real reasons behind certain decisions. Otherwise, they risk running into the classic trap of suggesting something, only to be met with a sigh and, "We tried that. It didn't work."

The Fastest Way to Build an Independent Team

At the end of the day, my goal as a manager isn't to have people popping into my office every five minutes asking, "Is this okay? What about this? Can you double-check this one more time?" I'm not trying to run a help desk. I want my team to move forward with confidence, knowing exactly what's expected of them and making smart decisions on their own. If I've mentored correctly, that's exactly what happens—I become less of a human FAQ and more of a strategic partner.

My responsibility isn't to dictate every tiny step of how something gets done. I'm not here to micromanage their every keystroke like some kind of corporate overlord. My job is to be crystal clear about the goal, the expectations, and the outcome. I hired this person because I believe they're capable, so I need to *let* them be capable. That's the whole point of mentoring. It's equipping people with the skills they need so you don't have to hover over their shoulder.

Where a lot of managers go wrong is in the how. It's tempting to jump in and say, "No, no, do it this way," but when we get too deep in the weeds of telling people exactly how to do things, we're not mentoring anymore, we're micromanaging. Few things kill confidence and motivation faster than micromanagement. If I've given clear expectations, taught the necessary hard skills, and outlined the desired outcome, then my job is to step back. Maybe they follow the process exactly as I taught it, maybe they find a better way. Either way, the work gets done, and I don't have to babysit every keystroke. That's a win. If something needs adjusting, I use scaffolding to guide the shift instead of hovering like a helicopter boss.

The reality is new employees are going to do things differently than I would. But different doesn't automatically mean wrong. The real question isn't "Did they follow my process?", it's "Did they get to the expected outcome?" If the answer is yes, let them be capable. That's literally why you hired them.

Don't forget that for the first few months, they're learning more than just their job. They're learning the people, the politics, the systems, and the unspoken rules of the company. Their brains are overloaded. Expecting them to operate at full speed right away is wildly unrealistic. Give them time. Trust is built in the space where we let people figure things out.

You'll likely wear the mentor hat for six months to a year with any new hire. After that, unless they're moving into a new role or taking on new responsibilities, you can retire it to the back of your managerial closet. Mentoring is temporary, but the independence it creates lasts. The goal is to build a team of people who don't need you watching their every move, so that eventually, they're the ones mentoring the next wave of employees while you focus on bigger things.

Chapter 10:
Wearing the Coach Hat

There comes a time in every manager's life when someone on your team walks into your office—or DMs you—with "hey, got a sec?" They're clearly wrestling with something. Maybe it's a sticky situation with a coworker. Maybe it's a decision about how to handle a project gone sideways. Either way, their eyes are basically saying, "Tell me what to do." This is where your coach hat comes in.

Now, before we dive into what coaching is, let's get really clear on what it's not. Coaching is not correcting. It's not teaching. It's not mentoring. And, this is the big one, it's not advice-giving. Not even if you have really, really good advice. I know it's hard. You've probably got a great story that would make this all make sense. But coaching is about holding space, not holding court.

The coach hat is for listening. For asking open-ended questions. For reflecting back what you hear so the other person can hear it too. It's about creating a mirror. When you're wearing this hat, the phrase *"What do you feel like your options are?"* is pure gold. Even better when followed with, *"And what are the pros and cons of those options?"*

In fact, when someone brings a situation to you, consider saying something like, *"Do you want advice, or should I wear my coaching hat?"* That little question gives them agency and gives you clarity. Because if they say, "I just need to talk this through," you've got your role. You're not the answer machine. You're the curious, compassionate coach.

Ted Lasso is a prime example of a great coach who doesn't need technical expertise to be deeply effective. The man didn't grow up playing football (and, let's be honest, still calls it soccer in his head), but he leads with empathy, curiosity, and a relentless belief in his team. He *chooses* to believe in their capabilities.

That's what coaching is. The more you do it, the more fulfilling it becomes. You'll start to see the people around you bloom in ways you didn't expect.

Coaching and the Stages of Change

Coaching is a lot like walking next to someone on a long, uneven trail. You're not pulling them forward. You're not pushing from behind. You're just there, asking questions, handing out water, and occasionally pointing out an alternate route when they hit a dead end.

Most managers want to fix things quickly. We see the problem, we've lived through the lesson, and we think, *If I could just get them to take this one step, they'd be so much better off.* And maybe they would. But change doesn't work like that.

This is where the Transtheoretical Model of Change comes in (try saying that three times fast).[47] It breaks down the process people go through when making a major shift—like quitting smoking, leaving a toxic job, or finally using their PTO. It's not linear, and it's definitely not fast. But understanding these stages makes you a much better coach.

Here's the breakdown:

---

[47] (Raihan & Cogburn, 2022)

1. **Precontemplation**—Not even thinking about change. Blissfully unaware or in denial.
2. **Contemplation**—Starting to wonder if maybe something needs to shift.
3. **Preparation**—Getting ready to do something about it.
4. **Action**—Actively making the change.
5. **Maintenance**—Keeping the change going.

Let's take a classic... the smoker friend. You've probably got one. They smoke with confidence, telling you they'll quit when they're dead. In contemplation, they say things like, "Yeah, I should probably quit someday." Preparation sounds like, "I'm going to quit on July 1st." Action is when they are white-knuckling their way through the first few days without a cigarette. Maintenance is them figuring out how to keep it going when stress hits or old habits creep in.

Most of the people we coach at work aren't in action yet. A lot of them are still *thinking* about thinking about it. If you try to coach someone in precontemplation like they're already in action, you're going to feel frustrated, and so will they.

Let's say someone is stuck in a job that's clearly draining the life out of them. You see it. They probably feel it. But they might still be saying things like, "It's not that bad," or "Every job has its problems." That's precontemplation. No plan. No urgency. Just coping. You're not going to get them to update their résumé at that moment, and trying to push them there will likely shut the conversation down.

What you *can* do is help them take the next step. Not the final step, just the next one. That might sound like asking, "What do you wish your day looked like?" Questions like this one are low-stakes. They don't require commitment. They invite reflection, and that's how people start to move. If they're in contemplation, you can shift toward preparation by asking, "If you decided to apply somewhere else, what kind of work would actually light you up?" In preparation, it becomes more tactical. That is where you ask, "Want to block an hour on Friday to sketch out your résumé?" or "Can I connect you with someone who's in a role you're curious about?" And if they hit action, you support the momentum without hovering by asking, "How's the search going?" or "What's surprised you so far?"

As their coach, you need to meet them at the stage they are currently at and help them slowly move forward. Keep in mind, people don't typically leap from "everything is fine" to "I'm changing my life" without some sort of catalyst. When it comes to the addiction community, this is typically referred to as their "rock bottom" moment. But this doesn't only come in addiction. These rock bottom moments can happen in careers when we get passed over for a promotion or get publicly shamed in a meeting. Or they could happen when you realize you dread waking up Monday mornings every single week. It's these moments that finally kick off the process of change.

But even then, it's rarely a straight shot. There's ambivalence and fear. As a coach, your job isn't to speed them up. It's to stay with them. Help them name what they want. Reflect back what you're hearing. Ask questions that gently challenge their assumptions. And most of all, trust the process. They'll get there. Just not always on your timeline.

One of the hardest lessons for any coach—or manager—is realizing that insight doesn't equal action. Just because someone knows something needs to change doesn't mean they're ready to change it right away. And that's okay. Change takes energy, courage, and often a sense of safety. Your job as a coach is to protect that spark while it grows, which requires you to sit with someone in their in-between when they're not ready to move, but no longer in denial. Rushing them never works here, but what does work is consistency, curiosity, and compassion. So, if you are doing all the "right" coaching moves and they still aren't taking action? Don't take it personally. You might have planted a seed that won't sprout for months. Either way, the seed is planted.

My Secret Ninja Move

If coaching had a black belt, it would be called Motivational Interviewing (MI). It sounds like something a therapist might whip out in a counseling session (and yes, therapists do use it), but so do coaches, and parents, and anyone who's ever tried to support another human being through a tough decision without telling them exactly what to do. Which makes it perfect for managers wearing the coach hat.

Motivational Interviewing is all about helping people find their own motivation to change by asking the right questions at the right time and listening to the answers.[48] When we use MI techniques, the hope is to help someone move from one stage of change to the next. For example, if someone is in the contemplation phase of change, we could help them move closer to the preparation phase.

I call this my secret ninja moves because it's your job to guide someone toward clarity while they think they are just talking. Done well, they won't even realize you're using tools. You're being curious, supportive, and asking thoughtful questions that slowly bring them closer to the decision they already wanted to make.

You don't need a certification to do this well. You need three things:

- Open-ended questions
- Active listening
- Sincere affirmations

Let's say one of your employees needs to have a hard conversation with a colleague. They've been avoiding it, but it's starting to affect the team. You could push them to do it. Or you could use MI techniques to help them want to. You might say, *"On a scale from one to ten, how motivated are you to have that conversation?"*

They say three. Instead of being disappointed, you celebrate it, *"That's great it's a three! Why a three and not a one?"* That question flips the conversation. It makes them articulate their own reasons for caring, and once they hear themselves say it, that three often starts to sound more like

---

[48] (Motivational Interviewing Definition Principles Approach, n.d.)

a five or six. Then you keep going, *"What are the options you're considering? What are the pros and cons of each?"*

These questions are invitations. They move people through the stages of change at their pace, while building trust along the way. If they ask you directly, "What do you think I should do?", the door is open. You can offer advice, because they've asked for it. But even then, keep it collaborative and say, *"I have a few thoughts. Do you want me to share them?"* That little check-in helps maintain the psychological safety of the moment. It reminds them that you're not steering the ship.

Motivational Interviewing works because it's built on respect. You're not pushing anyone to be something they're not. You're helping them uncover the reasons they want to grow in the first place and (once more) meeting them exactly where they are. No pressure. No performance. Just presence, patience, and a few well-placed ninja moves.

The Root of Coaching

Real listening (the kind that requires focus, presence, and zero multitasking) takes effort. It's a choice, and it starts before the conversation even begins.

If you're sitting in the office and your Slack notifications are pinging incessantly, turn off the screen and mute your speakers. If you're working from home and your dog is staring at you like he's about to spill company secrets unless you throw the ball, put him outside the room. To listen well, you need to create a space where you can focus.

This could mean deciding that for the next ten minutes (or thirty), this human in front of you gets your full attention. No open tabs or mental to-do checklists. Just you and them, figuring out something together. Once the space is there, the next move is mirroring. This is where most managers want to jump to "fix it" mode. Resist the urge! Instead, reflect back what you're hearing.

Let's say someone comes to you with this string of life chaos. They say, "Someone at work is spreading rumors about me, my roof is leaking, my fridge died, and this morning I got a flat tire." Your response? *"Wow! So, I'm hearing that there's some drama at work, your house is falling apart, and your car joined the party too. That's a lot. No wonder you're wiped."* This response is more powerful than our usual, "That sucks," because something shifts in their brain when they hear their own story reflected back. It's like holding up a mirror to their stress. Suddenly, it's not something they're surviving. It's something they can see clearly. Labeling the chaos makes space for validation. It also paves the way for better decisions.

When we're in the middle of the mess, we're usually too busy trudging forward to notice how heavy the load is. But when someone reflects it back accurately and empathetically, it opens the door for clarity. From clarity, we can make actual choices.

Of course, this trick doesn't only work for the rough patches. It works in the good times too. If someone casually mentions that they just booked the trip of a lifetime and their partner surprised them with front-row concert tickets, don't let that slide by unnoticed. Reflect it back. I'd say something like, *"Hold up—you're telling me you've got the dream vacation booked and a partner who's winning gold in the surprise gift Olympics? That's amazing. Are you letting yourself feel how good that is?"*

People, especially in work mode, tend to downplay joy. We normalize the hard stuff and gloss over the good. As a coach, you get to help them lean into the joy. Let them hear how beautiful their life sounds when someone else says it out loud.

That's really what coaching comes down to—making space and helping people actually *hear* themselves. You're not there to fix, rescue, or jump in with a brilliant solution. You're there to be present. To say, "Yeah, that's a lot," or "Wow, that's pretty great," and mean it. When people feel seen, they stop powering through on autopilot and start making clearer, more intentional choices.

Coaching Moments Can Be Brief

Not every coaching moment needs to be penciled into a calendar or opened with "So, what's on the agenda today?" In fact, some of the most impactful coaching happens between meetings in those moments when someone casually drops a thought your way without even realizing it's something they need help sorting out.

It might be a comment in the hallway. A throwaway line on a call. A Slack message that reads more like a sigh than a question. These moments don't come with a neon sign that say, *"Coach me now!"* but they're often the moments people are the most open. There's no pressure. No performance. Just a quiet opening and your choice about what to do with it.

You don't need to turn it into a full-blown coaching session. Sometimes it's as simple as one well-placed question. Or a short reflection. Or even making the space to let them keep talking, without rushing to the next thing. These moments are easy to overlook. They don't look or feel important. But over time, they create a rhythm, a dynamic where people start to trust that you're available, that you're curious, and that you're not only here to direct traffic. Instead, you want to walk alongside them when they need it.

So, while one-on-one meetings and structured conversations matter, don't underestimate the power of the quick check-in, the side comment, the passing "got a sec?" Those moments count. When you show up for people with presence and curiosity, these moments become something bigger than they seemed.

For many managers, in those moments, it's tempting to just tell them what you'd do. It would be faster. Cleaner. Maybe even appreciated. But what actually helps them grow isn't your answer, but the process of finding their own. So instead, you ask questions. You let them talk it through. You nudge them toward clarity. You show, in the subtlest way, that you trust their thinking and that you believe they're capable of making good decisions. Even when it's easier to just solve it for them, you resist that urge.

When the conversation wraps, whether it lasted five minutes or forty-five, you take a second to mirror it back. Not only what they said, but what they're going to do with it. You name the challenge they're navigating. You reflect the solution they've chosen. Then you ask how you can support them moving forward and when they want to check in again.

These micro-moments matter more than we think. They're quiet, often unplanned, and they build accountability, confidence, mutual respect, and trust over time. That is the kind of return on investment which doesn't directly show up in your metrics but absolutely shows up in your team's culture.

The Sweet Spot for Autonomy

If coaching had a secret ingredient, it would be autonomy. Remember when we talked about intrinsic motivation in chapter five? And how psychology researchers Deci and Ryan figured out that to be truly motivated you need autonomy, competence, and relatedness?[49] This is where coaching shines. Because coaching isn't about pushing an agenda or enforcing a policy. It's about meeting someone exactly where they are and walking alongside them while they figure out where they want to go. Coaching is pure autonomy in action. It's zero about you and one hundred percent about them.

Let's say you're managing a team and your department's goal is to hit a million dollars in sales. You already have a couple of ideas on how to get there. Rather than dropping the plan like a decree from the mountain, you bring the team into it. You say, *"Here are two solid strategies I've been considering. Which one do you think makes the most sense for us right now?"*

What you've done is given them a framework, but within that, you've offered choice. That choice is where buy-in lives. Nobody likes being told what to do. But ask someone what they think should be done, and suddenly they're engaged. They're leaning in. They're owning the outcome. Understanding these motivational roots gives us sharper tools for coaching. It helps us frame better

---

[49] (University of Rochester Medical Center, 2025)

questions and reminds us to focus less on control and more on partnership.

Your Input Is Not Needed

Not giving advice is hard. It feels unnatural at first. Like trying to hold back a sneeze or walk past a laughing baby without making a silly face. We're wired to want to fix and feel useful. And advice feels useful. It's the verbal equivalent of reaching out a hand. But in coaching, it's often more helpful to keep your hands, and your opinions, to yourself.

This doesn't come naturally for most of us. It's a learned behavior. Like anything worth learning, it takes practice, patience, and probably a few awkward moments where you catch yourself mid-sentence thinking, "Wait… nope. Not my turn."

When you're in coaching mode, your goal is to help people find their way forward, not hand them a pre-assembled map. That means letting go of the urge to "should" on them. You know the feeling: They *should* just talk to their boss. They *should* stop overthinking it. They *should* set better boundaries. Or worse: I *should* be giving them more guidance. I *should* know how to help. I *should* have better answers.

Stop "shoulding" on yourself. It's messy. It's unhelpful. And it rarely leads to clarity. Coaching is about helping people name what they want, not what they (or you) think they "should" want. That distinction matters. Now, if you're someone who's deeply trained in advice-giving (hi, most humans), it might take some rewiring to shift out of that mode. That's normal. And it's okay to ask for help. In fact, I recommend it.

Let the people around you know you're working on developing your coaching style. Tell your team, your partner, your roommate, your kids, or whoever's in your orbit that you're trying to break the habit of giving unsolicited advice. Give them permission to call you out when it slips through.

Even better? Give your advice-gremlin a name. Mine is Sandra. So, when I start to veer into "let me tell you what I would do" territory, someone can gently (or not-so-gently) say, "Hey… Sandra came out. Can you put her away?" It sounds silly. But it works. It reminds us, in real time, that the goal isn't to be right or helpful in the way we define it, but to support the person in front of us in the way they actually need. Sometimes, that support looks like saying less, asking better questions, and giving Sandra the day off.

Chapter 11:
Wearing the Supervisor Hat

This hat reminds us that yes, we are leading people, but we're also operating inside a business. Whether it's a nonprofit, a government agency, or a start-up duct-taped together with caffeine and optimism, every workplace has expectations, deliverables, and standards that matter. When we wear the supervisor hat, we're not just cheerleading, we're aligning people to those expectations so the work gets done and the mission stays on track.

That alignment shows up in all sorts of unglamorous but necessary ways—from recruitment and selection for projects, to navigating performance plans, to upholding the systems and structures that create a healthy work environment. This role demands professionalism and asks for clarity. But that doesn't mean we lose our warmth. You can be kind and still be direct. You can be human and still hold standards.

In terms of recruitment, it's where we pause and ask who has the right skills, experience, and values to help our team thrive. Not just who we'd want to grab tacos with on a Friday night (though, bonus if they check that box too). It's about being thoughtful, intentional, and aligned with the larger vision. You're not mentoring a potential hire. You're not their friend. You're assessing if they align with your mission, if they can do the job, and if they will contribute to the team's success.

The supervisor hat also comes out when performance doesn't meet the expectations we've co-created, or when someone's behavior starts impacting the whole team. In my own management style, I usually reach for the coaching or mentoring hat first. I want to believe that with the right support, people will rise. But sometimes, that's not enough. Sometimes, despite the best intentions, the team's morale dips because someone's slacking while earning the same paycheck as everyone else. Equity gets out of balance. In those moments, the supervisor hat is required.

This is where you might have to reach into your managerial utility belt and pull out the dreaded PIP (Performance Improvement Plan). The goal here isn't to punish anyone or play corporate cop. It's to bring clarity. A PIP is a structured way of saying, "These are the values we stand by, and we need your actions to start standing with them." If the issue is behavioral, like someone constantly clashing with the culture you're trying to cultivate, this is even more reason to create a PIP. But if it's only a singular missed deadline or one rough week? We keep coaching. We keep asking questions. We keep trying. Let's take a closer look at how to wear the supervisor hat with confidence and care.

Wear the Hat No One Wants with Grace

Of all the hats, the supervisor hat might be the one we dread the most because it often means we're stepping into conversations that are deeply uncomfortable. These are the moments where we carry messages no one wants to hear. Performance issues. Hygiene concerns. Terminations. These aren't exactly the highlight reel of leadership.

No one wakes up excited to say, "Hey, your work isn't meeting expectations," or "We need to have a chat about something... personal." It's uncomfortable. It's awkward. It makes you wish you'd called in sick, and yet these conversations are a necessary part of the job. If you're doing your job well, they shouldn't be a surprise.

When someone's performance is slipping, the seeds of change should have already been planted. First with the mentor hat, guiding them on what needs to be done. If that doesn't land, the coach hat steps in to explore what's beneath the surface and asks if there is something getting in the way. And if you have an established friend hat, you might lean on that too. But often, especially with newer team members or those where that relationship hasn't developed, it's time to put on the supervisor hat.

This is when you say, clearly and kindly, *"Your behavior or performance is not aligned with the expectations of this role."*

Notice the focus there: it's not on the person. It's on the behavior. On the outcomes. On the professional standards you've set. That distinction matters. We're not attacking identity; we're clarifying expectations. We are defining what is expected in this space and explaining that we are not seeing those expectations being met.

This conversation should come from a place of care. You can, and should, express that you are having this conversation because you see value in them. You can say, "I'm bringing this up because I care about your growth. Because I don't want this behavior to hurt your future, or to hurt the team we've worked so hard to build."

Supervising is about protection. Protection of the team's morale. Protection of the work. Protection of the individual in front of you, who might just need someone to tell them the truth with grace.

When we've done the work ahead of time—coaching, mentoring, offering feedback—it builds a bridge toward these harder moments. The individual knows there's been a struggle. They've felt the tension. They've been on a performance improvement plan. They've had support and resources offered. So, when the moment comes for that serious conversation, they don't walk in shocked. They walk in knowing. They may not be happy, but they understand. That's the real flex of a human-centered leader: not ducking the hard talks, but making sure no one walks into them feeling blindsided or bulldozed.

Write It Like the Whole Company's Reading

Sometimes the supervisor hat isn't about confrontation or performance improvement plans. Sometimes it's just... paperwork. Glorious, soul-sapping, eternal paperwork.

I'm talking about evaluations. Reviews. The institutional "stuff" that gets typed into systems, saved forever, and occasionally pulled back out when your employee is applying for another job or trying to get a raise. These things might not feel high-stakes at the moment, but trust me, they are.

Let me put it plainly. What you write in a formal evaluation is not just a comment in passing. It's not a sticky note. It's not a group chat vent. It's a permanent record. In many organizations, it's a record that can and will be requested by another department or hiring manager down the road.

So let me offer you this mantra: *Write like it's going in stone.*

If your employee has had one rough meeting but has otherwise been a consistent contributor, maybe skip mentioning that time they bombed the presentation. If they missed a deadline, but you've already addressed it and seen improvement, let it go. The evaluation is not a diary. It's a formal artifact. Use it to highlight their achievements, not nitpick their stumbles. Give examples of the real impact they've had. Share the data that shows how their work helped your team meet goals. Make the record reflect the *truth of who they are*, not just their worst moment this year.

I spent a chunk of my career knee-deep in systems, learning which fields get saved and which don't. (Spoiler alert: the important stuff always sticks.) Documents like PIPs and annual evaluations? Those suckers are saved. Forever. In digital amber. And they are read by people who don't know the full story or witness the growth that came from challenges. That's why the words you choose matter. It matters for raises, for bonuses, for promotions, and for cost-of-living increases. I want everyone on my team to be eligible for the most they can get, and as their supervisor, I see myself as their advocate, not their evaluator.

Let me give you an example. I once worked with a woman who shared vulnerably with her manager that she wanted to work on her communication style. She felt she came across a little blunt and was hoping to polish that up. It was a thoughtful, self-aware reflection. But her manager took that moment of trust and twisted it. In the woman's annual review, the manager wrote something to the effect of, "She is going to work on not being as blunt or rude." Not only was that unnecessary, it was a betrayal. And it lives on, in her permanent file, speaking volumes to people who were never in the room.

If someone is not actively underperforming, and if you're not trying to create a paper trail that supports their exit, then keep the formal reviews 100% positive. Save the constructive feedback for the real conversations, not the permanent documents. Say the hard things face to face. Use the eval to advocate for them.

Also, temper your expectations on paper. If someone sets a goal to bring in five-hundred-thousand dollars in donor revenue, and then the world shuts down in a pandemic, do you really want that failure recorded forever in black and white? Of course not! So, here's what I do: I cut the written goal in half. You tell me the real goal, and I'll write something fifty percent safer in the file. That way we build a cushion, and we don't set anyone up to fail on paper. Your job is to undersell the document and over-support the human.

For the record, I don't even believe in annual evaluations. Shocking, I know. I believe in *conversations.* Ongoing ones weekly or monthly. The kind where nothing in the "official" review is a surprise. If you're managing well, they already know what they're doing well and what needs work. So, when you get to the formal review, you can say, "Thank you. You've been awesome. Let's keep going."

I like doing seasonal or project-based reviews. For my business clients, I sit down with them quarterly and we do a bullseye activity. We map out what's hitting the target, what's around the edges, and what's way off base and needs fixing. It opens a clear, objective discussion around performance without the sting of judgment.

In education settings, we might do this as a half-day retreat. We'll mix in some training, some team-building, and then wrap with an evaluation of the semester. What worked? What didn't? What do we want to try differently next time? Then we tuck that info away to guide the next season.

The point here is rhythm and reflection. You don't have to wait until someone's floundering to give them feedback. In fact, you shouldn't. A great supervisor checks consistently, not just because the organization says so. When you keep the conversation consistent, it keeps the "elephants in the room" from growing into full-blown stampedes.

Create Systems of Support

Not everything about the supervisor hat has to be scary or sterile. Sometimes, it's just showing up consistently and creating a system that gives people a voice. For me, this is where monthly one on ones come in.

Let me be clear, this is not a luxury. This is the baseline. If someone is a full-time professional on your team, they deserve *at least* an hour of your time every single month. Not just when things go sideways. Not just when you've got an opening on your calendar and a spare moment between back-to-back chaos. Every. Single. Month.

For part-time folks? Once or twice a year might be enough. But full-timers? You owe them your presence. Your curiosity. Your attention. You owe them a seat across from you (whether it's at a coffee shop, on Zoom, or tucked in a quiet corner of the office) and a safe space to reflect on their work.

These one on ones aren't about checking off boxes or giving them a performance grade. They're a space to ask, what's been working? What are you proud of? What did you learn from that last project? What would you do differently next time?

Most people are deeply aware of what didn't go well, and they'll tell you. You don't have to point out the flaws. In fact, if you do, you risk putting them on the defensive, making them feel small, or triggering a shame spiral that makes real growth harder. Instead, let them lead the reflection. When someone says, "I think I'd plan for more buffer time next time," you don't need to say, "Yeah, I was going to mention that." Just smile and nod. Celebrate the insight and say, "Love that. Let's build that in."

This is a quiet kind of power. The supervisor hat doesn't always have to be commanding. Sometimes it's best worn while listening with intention and offering the gentlest of nudges. And yes, sometimes these meetings involve wearing a little bit of the coaching hat. You're asking the reflective questions, not prescribing the fixes. These conversations should feel collaborative, not corrective.

Let's say you hear from another team member that during a recent storage room reorganization, one of your employees had a big emotional day and was aggressively throwing supplies around in a way that made their teammates feel unsafe. Clearly, that's not okay. But instead of storming in like a hall monitor with a clipboard, you bring it up in your next one on one.

You might start simply by asking, "How did reorganizing the storage room go?" and then let the silence do some work. If your relationship is solid, they might say something like, "Well... I was having a rough day." Perfect. That's your opening. Then you can explain how their behavior impacted others by making them feel unsafe and ask how they would feel if the roles were reversed. Give them a chance to reflect. To self-regulate. To reconnect with your shared workplace norms. If this kind of outburst ever happens again? Then you shift back into the clear boundaries of your supervisor hat and say, "This isn't appropriate behavior in the workplace, and we need to see something different moving forward."

But again, even in these moments, it's not personal. It's not about *them*. It's about the behavior, the culture, and the safety of the space you're all sharing.

Let me share one more example. One of my clients had employees who wore very heavy fragrances. While no one smelled bad, some of their teammates (and guests) were allergic or sensitive to the smell. Instead of making it about personal hygiene (which would've been mortifying), we crafted a new team policy. Unscented products only. If you're wearing something scented, it should not have a scent radius bigger than two feet. Simple. Fair. Respectful. And importantly, we rolled it out gently in a weekly digital update. It acted as a quiet nudge toward a more inclusive space.

These are the moments where leadership gets subtle. Remember, you don't always need a separate, formal meeting for every issue if you're having regular, intentional conversations. That monthly one-on-one meeting is your pressure valve. It keeps tensions from building up. It invites people to share before things spiral. It gives you space to course-correct behavior without turning it into a spectacle.

At the end of the day, your job as a supervisor is to build an environment where people feel seen, safe, and supported. That takes time, consistency, and a whole lot of humanity.

Supervisor Is Not the Default

No one dreams of becoming a supervisor so they can have tough conversations, manage paperwork, and gently tell someone to stop throwing office supplies like dodgeballs. Yet, for many managers, this is the only hat they think they are supposed to wear. But that's a myth. A cultural holdover. And in most environments, it's wildly unhelpful.

Now, are there some spaces where this hat gets worn more often? Absolutely. Public works is a great example. You've got highly skilled, task-based staff operating in a traditional hierarchy, the workers and the supervisors. In those spaces, relationship-building might take a backseat to logistics. The friend hat doesn't always fit, and the coach hat may not be welcomed. There, the supervisor hat does more of the heavy lifting, and that's okay.

But for most office environments? For the teams made up of knowledge workers, creatives, admin staff, nonprofit professionals, and people juggling a million unseen tasks? The supervisor hat should not be your default. It's the hat you pull out when the others aren't working. When performance is off track. When the policies demand it. Or when you've already tried mentoring, coaching, guiding, and still, something isn't aligning with expectations. It's important. But it shouldn't be constant.

Yes, it's uncomfortable. *Of course it is.* Most of us don't grow up having to wear this kind of hat in our daily lives. We don't sit down with our friends to tell them they're underdelivering on shared goals. We don't file monthly reports on our siblings' interpersonal growth. So, the muscles required to wear the supervisor hat are new and a little shaky.

This hat also carries some fear. What if they hate me? What if they quit? What if this ruins the relationship? And let's not ignore where that fear comes from, it's often rooted in fear of abandonment, rejection, and being the "bad guy." It makes sense. But it's also not a good enough reason to stay silent. Correcting behavior protects the group.

If someone's actions are disrupting morale, breaking team trust, or clashing with the values you're building, saying nothing doesn't keep the peace. It just shifts the damage somewhere else. The rest of the team feels it. They start wondering if anyone cares. Slowly, that amazing culture you worked so hard to build starts to erode.

So, have the conversation. Even if it's hard. Even if your voice shakes. Even if it makes you sweat through your blazer. Correcting misalignment is a gift. It keeps the team safe and preserves the vibe. It ensures the whole team can continue to thrive.

In a perfect world, you've worn your mentor, coach, and friend hats often enough that the supervisor hat only makes cameo appearances. It's the "break glass in case of emergency" hat that you reach for when something's gone sideways or when the corporate landscape requires it. But if you're living in this hat every day, something's off. Either you're not using the other hats enough, or the team needs an adjustment. Let the supervisor hat be what it's meant to be: a clear tool used when needed, not a default identity.

Chapter 12:
Wearing the Friend Hat

The friend hat is the most misunderstood, often misused, and occasionally disastrous of all the managerial headwear. Unlike the others, this one doesn't come standard with the job. It must be earned, slowly, over time.

Just because we work together doesn't mean we're friends. I know, this is hard for some of us to hear. Especially managers that lean hard into the friend hat to try and make others like them. Friendship isn't a box you check on an onboarding form. It's built through trust, shared experiences, and the sheer endurance of surviving a full year of staff meetings together. It's not a job title, a perk, or a requirement. It's something that happens only when enough marbles have been placed in the trust jar.

Now, that doesn't mean we shouldn't be friendly. You absolutely should. Be approachable. Be kind. Engage in the occasional small talk about someone's oddly intense obsession with their sourdough starter. But recognize that not everyone you work with is destined to be more than that. Some coworkers will remain acquaintances who you exchange nods with at the coffee machine or suffer through icebreaker activities with. Others might be your go-to for lunchtime debates about whether Die Hard is a Christmas movie (it is, and I will not be taking questions), and that's perfectly fine.

The point is that friendship at work should be intentional, not automatic. By the time a year has passed, you've likely seen how your colleagues react under stress, whether they're a meeting interrupter or a meeting avoider, and how they handle the tragedy of a broken office coffee machine. You've seen their patterns, including the good, the bad, and the "Should I avoid their desk after three pm?" vibes. Only then can you decide, with full awareness, whether this is someone you'd genuinely call a friend.

Earned, Not Assigned

Friendship isn't automatic outside of work, so why would it be inside of work?

The friend hat is the result of building that trust. It's what happens when we've earned the right to be vulnerable with each other. As a manager, that might look like noticing something is off with someone and having the relationship to ask, *"Hey, you've been quieter than usual. Is everything okay?"* This hat allows you to recognize when something is out of the norm and ask about it on a personal level.

As a team member, before we reach this level, we might answer the above question with a vague response like "Oh, just some stuff going on at home." But once trust is truly there, the conversation shifts and our answer might change to the truer, deeper issue, "My sister is in rehab again."

But it doesn't mean we suddenly become weekend brunch buddies or start planning matching tattoos. It simply means that we've put enough marbles in each other's trust jars that we've earned the right to be more vulnerable with one another than we had before.

Now, sometimes, wearing the friend hat means showing up outside of work. Though this is rare, it's not unheard of. For me, I typically wouldn't attend a coworker's daughter's school musical if we were casual colleagues. But if we've worked together for years, and if I was there when she nervously told me she was pregnant, if I watched her navigate the chaos of early motherhood, then, yeah, I would want to be there. I care, and I'm invested in her journey as a person.

Leadership Isn't About Distance

As managers, we set the tone. If I want my team to feel safe sharing with me, I go first. That doesn't mean dumping my life story on them in week one. It means starting small, testing the waters, and gradually leveling up over time.

Remember our levels of vulnerability? You don't leap from level one to level four overnight. You start at level one, casual, safe, surface-level conversations. Then, maybe you push into level two where you share a bit more about your experiences, opening the door for real connection. And only after you've built that trust and you've seen how they respond, do you consider moving further. Realistically, it takes years for a work relationship to evolve into a genuine friendship. It'd say it takes two years, at least, to build the kind of connection where both people feel comfortable showing up as their full selves.

That slow build matters. It's what teaches us how to communicate life events professionally. It's how we learn when and how to share, so that when we do, it strengthens the relationship instead of making things weird. Yet, so many leaders believe they should not be friends with their team. They think that distance equals authority and friendship will make it harder to get people to follow their lead. That's simply incorrect.

The reality is that people are more likely to do what you need them to do when they care about you. Not because they're being forced to, but because they *want* to. They respect you, they value the relationship, and they don't want to let you down.

Now, does this mean friendship in the workplace requires late-night drinks and swapping messy dating stories? No. It's not about turning the office into a social club; it's about mutual care. Friendship, at its core, means that we genuinely want good things for each other. Not every work relationship will reach that level, and that's okay.

As we build deeper trust, we start noticing how people respond when we share. Do they listen without judgment? Do they offer support instead of unsolicited advice? Or do they shut down, dismiss, or make us feel like we shouldn't have shared at all? I know if I feel judged when I open up, I won't do it again. If someone makes me feel othered in that moment, I'll take it as a sign that our relationship isn't meant to go deeper. And that's not a failure, it's just information. Not every work relationship needs level four vulnerability. Some will always stay at level one, and that's perfectly fine.

The goal isn't to make everyone your friend. The goal is to create enough trust that the people around you feel safe, seen, and supported, wherever that relationship happens to land.

You Don't Have to Feel Alone Anymore

Management can be lonely. It's like being at a party where everyone's having a great time, but you're the designated driver. You're responsible for making sure everything runs smoothly, and there's often a feeling that you need to keep a certain level of distance. That's where the friend hat changes the game.

When we reach this level of trust with our team, we don't have to feel alone anymore. We get to work in an environment where we feel psychologically safe. Where the people we spend the majority of our waking hours with are allies instead of just colleagues.

A workplace where we genuinely like each other is more effective. When our relationships are meaningful, motivation increases, honesty is easy, and we're more likely to bring our full selves to the job. We're no longer just clocking in. We're showing up for each other. And let's be honest, it's a hell of a lot more fun to celebrate wins with people we enjoy than to sit through another forced, awkward office lunch where everyone claps halfheartedly over a grocery store sheet cake. Research backs this up. A study by BetterUp found that a high sense of belonging was linked to a fifty percent drop in turnover risk.[50] And research from Great Place To Work revealed that employees who experience belonging are five times more likely to want to stay at their company for a long time.[51] If we spend so much of our lives at work, wouldn't it be nice to enjoy our co-workers?

Afterall, we all get one-hundred sixty-eight hours in a week. If you're working a standard eight to five job with a commute that stretches your day from seven am to five pm, that's fifty hours a week dedicated to work. Now let's

---

[50] (Gonzales, 2022)
[51] (Bond, 2022)

factor in sleep. If you're getting a solid eight hours a night, that's fifty-six hours gone.

What's left? Not much. By the time you handle the bare-minimum functions of human life, including showering, eating, grocery shopping, basic chores, maybe exercising if you're feeling ambitious, you're left with maybe two to three hours a day for quality time with the people you love. That's less than half the time we spend at work.

Now, take a second and measure this for yourself. Track your hours. Look at how much time you're spending on work versus the people and things you care about. Most of us? We're not spending forty hours of quality time with our loved ones. We're spending it at work. So, shouldn't that time mean something? Wouldn't it be better if we were surrounded by people we trust, respect, and genuinely enjoy?

Welcome to the Space Where Open Communication Happens

The friend hat isn't about knowing who prefers cold brew over caramel lattes. It's about creating a space where real, unfiltered conversations can happen. When we get this right, we get access to our team members' actual *career and personal goals.*

If I've built enough trust to wear the friend hat, I want to know what's next for those on my team. Where do they see themselves in five years? (And no, I'm not asking this in a cringey job interview way.) When we truly care about our people, we don't panic when they start dreaming about their future. We get jazzed for them. We want to help them get there, whether that's within our company or beyond it.

If we don't have this level of trust, we don't hear about our employee's career aspirations until they're dropping a two-week notice on our desk. And let me tell you, that's not the ideal way to find out someone's been rethinking their future.

Case in point, I had a client's employee text me panicked, saying they'd received an offer from their old employer and didn't know how to tell their boss. Now, had we built the right level of trust, this would have been the perfect moment for an open, strategic conversation. Instead of jumping ship immediately, we could have talked through options. So, I told them, "Hold up. Just because you got an offer doesn't mean you have to take it. Take the weekend to process. Show me the offer. I can help you negotiate. Or, if you love where you're at, we can explore a counteroffer."

Did they take my advice? Nope. They resigned with zero conversation, no negotiation, and just peaced out. That dumped the entire marble jar on the floor. The irony was both their manager and I actually *wanted* to be excited for them. We'd invested time and energy into their growth, and we wanted to celebrate this next step. But instead of a high-five and a well-planned transition, we got radio silence and a scramble to fill their role.

This is why the friend hat matters. When we've earned it, we get to know things we wouldn't otherwise, like career ambitions, long-term goals, and personal transitions. That gives us time to plan, to train, and sometimes, to craft a role that meets their evolving needs so good employees don't have to leave. Even when they do move on, it doesn't have to be a loss. When the relationship is built on trust and open communication, we remain valuable to each other long after the exit interview. They move forward with our full support, and we gain an ally, maybe even a future business connection, instead of just another former employee.

That's a win for them. That's a win for us. That's a win for the entire organization.

Addressing a Change in Baseline

I hope I've made it clear that leadership isn't only about tasks and deadlines—it's about people. People have patterns. When those patterns shift (when the usually engaged team member seems distant, or the reliable one starts missing details), something is going on. This is a time to put on the friend hat so you can respond with care instead of control.

A simple, *"Hey, I've noticed you're a little quiet this week. How's it going?"* can be all it takes to open the door. If you've built trust and have put enough marbles in the jar, this moment can be an opportunity for them to feel seen, to know someone cares.

These conversations don't have to feel stiff or forced. Sometimes, the best way to check in isn't in a formal sit-down across a desk but in a casual, low-pressure setting. If there's a coffee shop nearby, take a walk, grab a cup, and let the fresh air and warm drink work their magic. Movement plus caffeine? It's practically a cheat code for deeper conversations. It gives them space to process, to share if they're ready, or at the very least, to know you noticed.

If they don't open up, that's okay. You've done your job by asking. Just because they aren't ready to talk today doesn't mean they won't be ready next week. If the shift in behavior continues, check in again. Patterns tell us a lot; so does consistency in showing up.

Advocating When a Change in Baseline Happens

Being a human-centered manager means recognizing when someone needs more than a quick check-in. Maybe they need a day or two to reset, a temporary shift to remote work, or simply a lighter workload while they navigate a tough situation. Sometimes, it's as simple as letting them know what resources are available, whether that's FMLA, employee assistance programs, or other HR benefits.

Remember, supporting your employees in tough moments is *always* better for them and the business. If you can find an accommodation that keeps a great employee on your team, that's a win for both of you. Losing someone, especially a good someone, means restarting the hiring, training, and onboarding process, which is an exhausting, expensive journey.

I once had an employee who was a new mom, and her plan was to return to the office after her FMLA leave. About two weeks into mom life, she called me, worried and overwhelmed. Her daughter had an immune disorder, and she wasn't sure she could come back at all. Now, I could have panicked, assumed I was about to lose a full-time employee, and started drafting a job posting. But instead, I said, "I hear you. If that's your decision, I support it. But we don't have to decide today. Let's take a beat and explore what you really need."

The solution? She needed to work remotely on Fridays. That one small adjustment made all the difference. You see, her daughter's grandmothers, who were her primary caregivers during work hours, weren't available that day, and traditional daycare wasn't an option due to the health risk. With one shift in her schedule, she got to keep her job, and I got to keep a valuable team member.

That's what it looks like to lead with patience. To say, "We don't have to make a decision today, let's figure out what works." Maybe part-time is an option. Maybe remote work is. Maybe a workload adjustment can keep them afloat. When employees feel cared for, they come back stronger, more engaged, and with even more marbles in the trust jar.

Not Every Moment Is a Friend Hat Moment

There are moments when the friend hat needs to take a backseat. It's not that friendship disappears. It's that certain situations demand a different hat. If we are about to present to the full leadership team, that's a leader hat moment, not a friend hat moment. If we're out with clients, handling a crisis, or leading a high-stakes meeting, those professional priorities take precedence over friend time.

If you're feeling like work has been all business lately, and you miss catching up with a work friend? Schedule time outside of work. There's no rule against grabbing dinner, going for a hike, or setting aside time to connect when the work calendar isn't dictating your every move, especially during a busy season when your usual coffee chats are getting replaced with back-to-back meetings.

But remember, like we mentioned in chapter five, whether you like it or not, you have power. With power comes perceived obligation. If we invite a team member to something personal, they might feel pressured to attend because they worry about how it could affect their opportunities at work. Maybe they're eyeing a promotion or hoping for a raise, and suddenly that invite to your birthday party feels less like a casual hangout and more like an unspoken test of loyalty.

That's why we need to be thoughtful about forming friendships across different levels of the organization. Our invitations carry weight, and we don't want to put our team in a position where they feel like saying no isn't really an option.

Work and personal life can overlap, but they don't have to. Some people prefer clear separation, and that's completely valid. Personally, I wouldn't invite colleagues to personal events unless we had a long history and a deep level of trust. I need to know that I can fully be myself in that setting, that I don't have to keep my leader hat on while I'm wearing my party hat. Because let's be honest, there are some things my team does not need to see, like me at a wedding after three glasses of champagne, living my best life on the dance floor.

The friend hat doesn't look identical across all levels of leadership. A CEO's work friendships will naturally have different dynamics than those of an entry-level employee. There's also the complexity of skip-level relationships—where a senior leader forms a direct friendship with someone several levels below them. That can create some interesting power dynamics, so it's worth being extra mindful in those situations.

At the end of the day, friendships at work should feel natural, not transactional. If they evolve, great. If they don't, that's okay too.

The Temporary Nature of Work Friendships

The reality of professional life is that people don't stay in the same job forever. Colleagues come and go, roles evolve, and team dynamics shift. Most direct teams will spend a few years together before someone moves on—and that's not a bad thing.

As leaders, we need to recognize this, not fear it. The friendships we build at work are valuable for what they are right now. They make work better, they make us stronger, and they help us grow. But we also need to acknowledge that when one of us leaves, the relationship will change. We won't see each other every day anymore.

But just because a working relationship evolves doesn't mean it has to disappear. Friendships (real ones) extend beyond a job title or an office space. If we've built this level of trust, we should honor it. That doesn't mean we suddenly have to become each other's new inner circle, but it does mean we can make the effort to stay connected in small but significant ways.

For me, that means keeping in touch. If a former colleague calls, I pick up. If they text, I respond. I make a point to check in at least once a year, even when life gets busy, even when everything keeps moving forward. Even though our day-to-day lives have changed, the relationship still matters. In a professional space, showing up for people can look different too. It might mean writing a letter of recommendation, being a reference for their next opportunity, or just being in their corner when they need career advice.

Work friendships may start in the office, but the best ones outlast job titles and team rosters. If we've put in the time to earn the friend hat, we should honor it, whether that means supporting each other in the workplace or staying in each other's corners long after we've moved on.

Chapter 13:

Wearing the Leader Hat

There's a point after the onboarding awkwardness, after the training, after the "Wait, who's responsible for this?" emails, where things finally settle. The team knows their roles. Trust is forming. Rhythm sets in. That's when you get to put on the leader hat.

Let me be clear, this hat isn't something you wear on day one. You earn it by mentoring, coaching, supervising, and occasionally showing up as a friend when life gets rough. Only after you've invested that time and effort does the leader hat truly fit.

Wearing it means facilitating a space where your team can identify problems, design solutions, and take ownership. People don't commit to what they're told. They commit to what they helped build. The leader hat is a privilege. It marks the shift from managing the to-dos to inspiring the what's next. From checking boxes to co-creating the blueprint. But it only works if you've done the work that comes before it.

It's tempting to want to put this hat on right away. Especially if you have read leadership books or listened to the podcasts that say, "Empower your people." Yes, empowerment is the goal. But leadership without trust feels hollow. If you haven't built real connections using the other hats, you haven't earned the right to lead them yet.

Trust is your highest currency. We need to be putting marbles in their jars through all the actions I've outlined in the other hats. Only when those jars are filled do we get to put this hat on. So, if you're eager to wear the leader hat, that's a good sign. It means you care. But slow down. Do the work first. Build the foundation. When the time is right, that leader hat will feel earned.

The Post-It Principle

Even when you put on the leader hat, problems will surface. They might not always be interpersonal; they could be due to a process change or new projects. But when those problems do surface, you shouldn't be the one to say, "We'll fix it this way."

I know that sounds wrong. Many managers think if they are the leader, they should have the solution to the problem. But when you wear the leader hat, you understand that people won't typically back or believe in a solution they didn't have a hand in making.

So, what do I do when something's off? First, I resist the urge to "fix it" myself, and instead, I gather the crew. We sit down and talk about the issue. In those meetings, my goal is to ask the right questions to help the team clearly articulate the real problem because if we can't name the issue, we certainly can't solve it. Once we've nailed the problem down—like, actually agreed on it in plain English (not jargon)—it's time for the fun part. Brainstorming solutions! This is where the Post-Its come in.

I give each person three sticky notes. Everyone writes down three possible solutions to the problem (yes, even the introverts and the overthinkers). The goal here isn't perfection. It's participation. Then we put those Post-Its up on a wall (or in a digital workspace, if you're remote) for us to review together. When I explain this method, many wonder why I don't just let the team verbally brainstorm the solutions. But when you do that, the introverts happily clamp their mouths shut and let the extroverts shout out ideas. This way, there are no interruptions, no talking over each other, no "let me piggyback on that" derailments, and everyone participates.

As we start looking at the sticky notes with solutions, we begin to organize them. Patterns typically start to show up. If five people wrote down some version of "our handoff process is trash." Great. That's data. That's not one person's gripe. It's a team-wide insight. I group similar notes together so we can see the trends. That's when the discussion starts and I ask, *"Which of these are doable? What's the time commitment? What's the budget? What's the lift?"*

Now, instead of pushing my brilliant idea, I'm facilitating a conversation that includes everyone's voice and lets the team weigh the pros and cons. Which then allows us to build a consensus. When you do this, you are leading by empowering, and the long-term impact creates a team that helps build, and fully backs, the solution.

After doing this enough, eventually, your team will start showing up with their own Post-It strategies. They start solving problems *before* you even get there. That's how you know you've successfully worked yourself out of the middle.

Once the solution is in play, don't vanish like a magician after the reveal. Circle back. Talk about how it went. Ask: What worked? What would we do differently next time? Yes, I'm calling us back to our monthly one on ones. From the amount of times I've brought them up, I'm sure you see why they are so important. With them, you keep the conversation going, and you can continue to facilitate as the team recognizes and solves problems together.

Work Yourself Out of a Job

If you're doing your job well as a leader, your team should eventually be able to run without you. I know. That stings a little. But leadership isn't about being indispensable; it's about building something that doesn't crumble the second you take a vacation (a real one, with airplane mode and fruity drinks).

Great leaders are always working themselves out of a job. When you lead well, you earn bigger roles, broader responsibility, and new challenges. That means someone else needs to be ready to step into your shoes.

If you ever played sports as a kid, you probably remember what it felt like to have a great team captain. Not someone who barked orders or tried to do everything themselves, but someone who kept everyone focused, encouraged, and moving in the same direction. That's what real leadership looks like. It's about setting a shared course, inviting your team into the process, and adjusting together when things change. When people feel trusted to help shape the path, they stay more engaged, more accountable, and more willing to give their best, even when the game gets tough.

So, you start looking. You notice who takes initiative, who others naturally follow, who asks the kinds of questions leaders ask. Then you start investing in them. You coach them, delegate stretch assignments, and give them space to grow so that when the next opportunity opens up for you, there's someone ready to take the baton without breaking stride.

If I'm leading a team and I know someone is killing it in their role, my brain is already asking, *What would it take to get them ready for mine?* And I want my managers to think the same way. You're not just running a store, a team, or a program. You're running a talent pipeline.

As we know, everywhere in corporate America, people leave, promotions happen, babies are born, people move, employees take sabbaticals, mental health breaks, or have family health crises they have to attend to—all of it is normal. *Turnover is not a crisis.* It's part of the cycle. But if you are not preparing for it, then every departure feels like an emergency.

Let's say your company decides to open a new location. Do you already know who's got the spark, the skills, and the trust equity to step into leadership? Or are you scrambling to train someone in two weeks while hoping they don't set anything on fire? If it's the latter, that's a signal. You need to identify future leaders now. Not after someone puts in their notice.

Start by asking:

- Who consistently takes initiative?
- Who do people turn to when they're stuck?
- Who models your team values without being asked?

Once you've got names, your next job is to invest. Mentor them. Coach them. Give them bite-sized leadership responsibilities. Let them run a meeting, lead a mini-project, and handle a tough conversation with your support.

Give them the training wheels before they need the mountain bike.

The goal here isn't to create clones of yourself. The goal is to create capable, confident humans who can step in when opportunity knocks or when life throws you a curveball. When the leadership bench is deep, the whole organization breathes easier. When the day comes that you get promoted, move on, or simply decide to take that sabbatical and finally write your memoir, you'll know your team is in good hands. And that? That is compassionate leadership that leaves behind a legacy.

Relationship Building Is Not an Option

As the leader, you're the one responsible for creating space where people can connect outside of their tasks. I'm not talking about team meetings (I've already covered that). This is about creating a space where people can interact, chat, and laugh about something other than work. Some organizations throw a holiday party once a year to check this box. Personally, I think that's a little silly. It feels like a tax write-off disguised as an attempt at joy. It's fine, but it's not what we're looking for here.

Turnover is real. Teams shift. People come and go. So, if we're only gathering once a year in a hotel banquet room with a cheese tray, awkward small talk, and a presentation by the CEO, we're missing the opportunity to actually build relationships. We need to get people together more than that for one sole purpose: connection.

I had one client take their whole team to see the musical Wicked. It became their yearly thing. It matched their brand, gave everyone something to look forward to, and most importantly, they were together having fun.

Another client organized an axe throwing night with pizza. There were about twenty of us, and we spent fifteen hundred dollars. It was completely worth it because the experience was joyful and weird, and it bonded us.

When you are leading a team, joy is always budgetable. Whatever your annual process is, plan for these kinds of events. Apply for a grant. Move a line item. Do what it takes. Because yes, you can buy Costco pizza and hang in the breakroom. But what you need is something that feels like a break from the routine. Something that sparks a different kind of conversation. Something that makes people feel like they belong.

Twice a year tends to be the sweet spot. These events don't have to be expensive, and they definitely don't have to be perfect, but they do need to be intentional. When we experience something new together, we bond faster. We build trust. We fill our energy cups. And those moments outside the normal routine are one of the best places to add marbles into the trust jar.

Every conversation that happens at one of these events adds a layer to your culture. It helps people feel more valued as human beings. When people feel valued, work improves. Conflict becomes easier to navigate. Tension gets diffused before it boils over because we know each other as people instead of just coworkers. We are more likely to give each other grace and more willing to engage honestly. These connections make everything easier.

So no, this isn't fluff. This is the glue. This is the real work of leadership. If nobody's planning it, that means it's yours to organize.

The Little Things Are the Big Things

Relationship building doesn't have to mean a six-month planning committee and a branded hashtag. Sometimes it looks like gathering your team for something that's just plain fun. Something that doesn't feel like work and doesn't ask anyone to bring a PowerPoint.

I've taken teams to escape rooms because you learn a lot about how people communicate under pressure when they're trying to decode a riddle with a fog machine going off in the corner. I've also done bowling, gone to driving ranges, and tried indoor rock climbing. What you choose depends on your people and your budget.

It might be something low-key and meaningful, like taking the team to a book signing for a title that's been a hit in your office. Or if you're feeling fancy, paying to bring in the author for a private Q and A. Maybe you've got a team that would light up at the idea of hitting their favorite dessert shop after a long week. Do the thing your people will actually enjoy. The thing that makes them feel seen and appreciated.

And listen, it doesn't always have to be an event. Traditions matter. They create memories. And memories create connection. The more shared experience we stack up, the closer we feel. The closer we feel, the stronger our trust becomes. So, if you don't have the budget for an event, look to create a tradition. Pajama Fridays or Door Dash coffee Mondays could be a great alternative. One of my personal favorite rituals is root beer float Fridays during the summer months.

Whatever you do, it doesn't have to be elaborate. It just needs to be new or different enough to break the routine. You don't have to book a charter bus or hire a magician. You could walk down to the bakery with your team and buy everyone a cookie. You could make hot chocolate in a crock pot with marshmallows and pass it around in mismatched mugs like I did once. It was simple. It was homemade. And people still talk about it. Those moments become part of your organizational history. They are the stories your team tells. The inside jokes that show up in meetings. The thing that makes someone say, "I love working here." When you prioritize moments like this, you build magnetism and the kind of culture that attracts the right people. Nothing says come work here like a group of humans who clearly care about each other.

Don't overthink it. Just do something together. Try something new. Laugh a little. Drink the hot chocolate. The trust you're looking for is often hiding in moments just like that.

Break Bread Often

I believe in the power of eating together. I believe in it the way some people believe in horoscopes or the healing magic of oat milk.

When we sit down and share a meal, something ancient and essential happens. It's in our cave-people bones. Our earliest human ancestors didn't gather to do a post-mortem on the third-quarter results. They gathered to share resources, survive the night, and connect over the fire. They ate together because it built trust and kept them alive. Weirdly enough, that hasn't changed.

We are still wired to bond over food. It doesn't have to be fancy. It doesn't have to be catered. But it does need to be intentional. As leaders, we need to create the space and time for it to happen. When we eat together, we talk differently. We share stories. We remember things. We get to see each other outside the context of deliverables and deadlines, and that's where real connections start to grow.

Now I don't call myself a foodie—though maybe I am—because I love a good Michelin-starred restaurant. I love what it represents. It's a meal that is curated like an *experience*. The head chef has thought through everything including how the food tastes, how it looks, how it smells. From the locally sourced ingredients to the lighting to the fabric of the napkins, it's all intentional. It's all designed to give you an experience you couldn't have on your own.

That's leadership. It's a curated experience that is designed to help you slow down, engage your senses, and become part of a shared experience. When you do that with your team, even once or twice a year, something shifts. Walls come down. Conversations go deeper. People feel cared about and cared for.

One of the best decisions I made with a client last year was pushing them to provide food during full-day training. They listened. We ordered lunch. Nothing fancy. Just good food, shared together. And everything changed. People's energy was better. They connected across departments. They stayed more engaged. It turned a long day into something people looked forward to. If you want to build psychological safety, start by asking what's for lunch. The rest will follow.

I know many of the strategies in this leader chapter were about gathering and connecting. That was intentional. Keep the management tasks for the other hats. When you wear your leader hat, your focus is facilitating problem solving and creating space for connection. If you have a full trust jar and bring people together frequently, you'll be amazed by how connected and engaged your team will become.

Chapter 14:

Deciding What Hat to Wear

Managing people requires knowing which version of yourself the moment needs. Some days, you're the calm presence in a storm. Other days, you're the motivator, the boundary-setter, the strategist, or the shoulder to lean on. Each situation asks for something different. If you try to lead every moment the same way, you'll either burn out or miss what your people really need. That's why I've introduced the hats to you. They may make the different aspects of management easier to picture, but choosing the right one is the difference between managing on autopilot and managing with intention.

You've likely worn all of these hats before. Maybe you were mentoring someone without calling it mentorship. Or stepping into leadership without realizing it. But knowing the hats isn't the same as using them intentionally. That takes practice. It means taking a beat when something comes up and asking, "What version of me does this situation need right now?"

This chapter is a bit of a costume change montage (cue the music). We're going to walk through real scenarios and explain the choice of hat used. There's no universal script, but there are cues to pay attention to, including what the moment calls for, what the person in front of you needs, and what your emotional intelligence is telling you. Let's dive in!

An Employee Tells You They Are Ready to Be Promoted (Coach Hat)

Almost every manager will experience an employee walking into their office to say, "I think I'm ready for a promotion" even though they have only been at your company… six months.

Now, the older and more seasoned we get, the more tempting it is to raise an eyebrow and say, "You're not ready." End of conversation. We might even have a whole list of reasons why that's true, including experience, maturity, scope of role, and the ancient managerial wisdom of "earning your stripes." But jumping straight to that answer, no matter how justified, usually leads to a LinkedIn job search.

What this employee has told you is their *proposed solution*, a promotion. What they haven't told you (yet) is the problem they're trying to solve. That's where your coach hat comes in.

Instead of shutting the conversation down, open it up. Get curious about what's underneath the request. Ask them what's motivating the desire for a promotion. Is it about money? A need for recognition? Are they craving more challenge or responsibility? Explore what they feel is missing in their current role. The goal is to understand what they are actually reaching for so you can help them find a path that truly fits.

In many of the organizations I work with (especially those with one hundred to two hundred employees), there aren't a lot of leadership spots. So, titles become the thing folks chase. My follow-up is often, *"Why that title? What are you really trying to do? What's the impact you want to have?"*

If you only respond with "you're not ready," they'll first feel hurt, and then they'll start looking for other jobs. But if you validate their ambition and invest in helping them grow, they're far more likely to stick around. Now keep in mind, this type of situation isn't a one-and-done conversation. It's usually the beginning of several. Your job is to help them unpack what they want, understand the limits of the current organization, and explore new ways to learn and grow.

Sometimes the answer isn't promotion, it's reinvention. That was the case for the manager in this scenario. He told me he was ready for a new role, but there wasn't anything open. As we dug into it, we realized he was bored. So, we brainstormed ways he could stretch himself, some work-related, some not (remember not all productivity has to come from your job).

For him, we found that he wasn't doing one on ones with his team, and that was a leadership muscle he wanted (and needed) to build. It scared him though, so we turned it into an action item. Eventually, we crafted a new job description together. We started with the question: *What problems do you see that you're excited to solve?* Then we let him pitch a role that matched those problems. That kind of clarity makes it much easier for leadership to say yes to the new role because money can be reallocated, titles can be adjusted, and vague ambition has now been translated into clear, strategic value. When someone brings that kind of moxie and momentum, your goal should be to keep their energy in the organization, not accidentally push it out the door.

Of course, not every story ends with a custom role and a coaching win. Sometimes, the person isn't a long-term fit. That's when this starts to edge into supervisor territory. If they are trying to grow in a direction your organization can't support, you can be honest and supportive about that. Help them apply elsewhere. Guide their exit with care. In organizations under ten thousand people, upward mobility can be limited. Some people need to leave to grow. Your job is to help them do that with clarity, dignity, and your full support.

When you get a promotion question like this, use the coach hat to talk them through the real problem underneath the ask. Chances are, you will surface new ways they can add value and feel more energized by the work they are doing.

An Employee Is Ready for a New Career (Mentor Hat)

Sometimes, unexpected conversations can turn into meaningful mentorship moments. One you'll likely encounter is when one of your employees drops this bombshell in your next one-on-one meeting: "I'm thinking about switching careers." Don't get angry, stop any feelings of betrayal in its tracks, and *breathe*. This doesn't have to be the end. It can be a beginning, and your first response sets the tone.

So, instead of panic or a poker face, try, *"Wow. Thank you for telling me! That's exciting. Tell me more."*

Because it *is* exciting. People don't make major career changes lightly. They've probably been dreaming, researching, and soul-searching for weeks before bringing this to you. So, before you start mentally adjusting team workloads or updating your org chart, meet them in the moment. Get curious. What industry are they looking at? What role sparked their interest? What got them thinking? Be someone who can say, "That's amazing," and mean it. Showing them you're in their corner, even as they step outside your world, builds trust that lasts far beyond their time on your team.

Once the celebration has had its moment, shift into the more practical stuff. Ask:

- Have you started applying yet?
- What's your plan or timeline?
- How are you preparing for this change?

This is where your mentor hat kicks in. You have experience they can lean on. As a leader, you likely sift through piles of résumés and conduct hundreds of interviews. You've seen the inner workings of hiring from the other side of the table. You can give them a leg up in the process. Offer to look at their résumé. Be a second set of eyes on their cover letter. Reframe your one on one to help them prep. If they're open to it, help them strategize how to tell their story in this new context.

If they have a particular company or industry in mind, that's a jackpot. Now you can dig into job boards, company websites, even LinkedIn org charts. When I'm helping someone find a job, I always advise them not to send résumés into the void. Send emails to humans instead. Find someone in the organization you might work with, and email them with something like, "Hey, I think your company's rad, and I'd love to learn more about your journey and what it's like working there." That email will get you *way more* replies than emailing in your résumé. It sparks real conversations. Maybe most importantly, it lets your employee audition the culture before they even apply.

Résumés might get you interviews (if the algorithm is feeling generous), but relationships build momentum. If the vibes are off in a coffee meeting? Great, they just dodged a bad fit. That's a win for everyone.

Before they officially start packing up their desk, there's one more question worth asking: *"Is there anything that would make staying an option?"* Sometimes, the answer is a firm no. Their heart is set, the dream lives elsewhere, and your job is to cheer them on as they go. But other times, this question opens up an entirely new conversation. Maybe they're bored and hungry for something different. Maybe they're feeling stuck in their current role and didn't realize a lateral move or stretch project was even possible. This is where the real mentoring magic happens—helping them explore whether their next chapter *must* happen somewhere else, or whether it could unfold right where they are, with the right support and structure.

At the end of the day, the goal of the mentor hat isn't to retain every employee forever. It's to be the kind of leader who walks alongside someone as they figure out what's next and supports them whether that next step is across the hall or across the country. You don't have to be the hero of their story. But you can be the manager who didn't flinch when they said, "I'm thinking about leaving," then leaned in, listened, and helped them rise.

An Employee No Calls No Shows (Supervisor Hat)

Every single one of us has been late to work at least once. So, it's fair to say that you'll likely experience an employee being late for their shift more than a few times as a manager. You will glance at the clock and realize that an employee who was scheduled at 8 am has yet to show up, and it's now thirty minutes past their scheduled shift time. You'll check your company communications and see no text, no email, and no sign of life.

This is officially in no-call, no-show territory. But, before you start crafting a mental termination letter, pause. Your response here will tell the employee whether you trust them or not.

Let's start with a new employee, someone you've known for less than six months. You don't have much context yet. You are still building the relationship, still figuring out who they are and how they communicate. Your first move shouldn't be punishment; it should be to check-in. Use the method they seem most comfortable with (text, Slack, email, whatever) and send something simple, human, and direct like, *"Hey [Name], worried about you. Had you on the schedule at eight am today. Are you okay?"*

They might've quit and not said anything. Or they might've overslept. You don't know. So don't come in hot—come in curious. If they don't reply that day, reach out again the next morning. Give them a gentle deadline, that might look like, *"Hey, we're still concerned. Please get back to me by five pm so we can figure out next steps."*

If silence continues? That's when you shift to a formal message the next day and say, *"Since we haven't heard from you, we won't be adding you to the schedule moving forward. If this was in error, please reach out by [Date/Time]."*

It's firm, it's fair, and it leaves the door cracked, just in case. But if this is an existing employee, someone you do know, someone with marbles in the trust jar, your response is going to look very different. Because your first thought shouldn't be "Ugh, they blew off work," it should be, "Oh no, something's wrong." In that case, I might send a message like, *"Hey [Name], you're not here and I don't want to say I'm freaking out... but I kind of am. Are you okay?"*

Notice the tone. There's no mention of the job. No guilt. Just care. In these moments, your job isn't to manage performance, it's to be a person. If they've built a track record of reliability, and they suddenly vanish, it's probably something big, like a loss, a car accident, or a crisis. And you don't need all the details right away. Often, they'll respond with a simple "I'm okay. I'll call later." Let that be enough for now.

Then, as you reconnect, show them what support looks like. If they're going to need time off, help them navigate leave policies or get the right paperwork. Advocate for what they need. Let them set the tone for what (if anything) you share with the team. And—if it feels right—rally some kindness. A meal. A note. A gesture that says "we've got you" can go a long way.

This is where assumptions can really mess us up. It's easy to jump to conclusions. But as the old saying goes, when you assume… well, you know the rest. In human-centered leadership, if you're going to assume anything, assume there's a reason. Assume something happened. Because if you assume someone's being careless or flaky, and you're wrong, you've just pulled marbles from the trust jar, and it's hard to earn those back. But when you lead with care (especially when it's hard), you make deposits into the trust jar. You show up as someone who sees the *human behind the job,* and that's a leader people want to come back to.

An Employee Is Being Bullied (Leader Hat)

Unfortunately, bullying doesn't only happen in schools. When someone on your team walks into your office and says, "I think I'm being bullied," your first job is not to investigate. It's to listen.

Because whether or not something meets the textbook definition of bullying, when someone tells you they feel hurt, intimidated, or unsafe, that's your signal to lean in, not debate the definition. In human-centered leadership, the experience of harm is equally as important as the intention behind it. You don't have to agree with every feeling to honor the fact that someone is having one. But when someone risks vulnerability to bring you a concern, especially something as heavy as bullying, you can't meet it with suspicion or skepticism. You need to meet it with empathy and curiosity.

Now, when it comes to behavior in the workplace, we often oversimplify. But it helps to understand the spectrum because not every hurtful interaction is created equal. First, there is rudeness. This is usually unintentional. It's a one-off. Someone interrupts you in a meeting, snaps under pressure, forgets to say thank you. It's awkward, maybe even a little hurtful, but it's not calculated. There's no agenda behind it, just a moment of stress or poor communication. We all do this sometimes. It's human.

Then there's mean comments. Mean is different from rude because it's deliberate. The comment was designed to sting. Maybe it was about someone's work. Maybe it got personal. It was purposeful, but isolated. That doesn't make it okay. But it also doesn't mean you're dealing with a toxic pattern. Sometimes mean behavior is someone lashing out during a rough patch. Still worth addressing, still worth a conversation, but likely repairable.

Bullying, though, is something else entirely. Bullying is consistent. It's patterned. And most importantly, it continues *after* the person on the receiving end has asked it to stop.[52] That's what distinguishes it from the other two. It's not a bad day. It's a bad behavior that has been flagged as harmful and keeps happening anyway. That's where you move from coaching and clarifying into corrective action. As the leader, you need to know which layer you're working with, but not before you first say, *"I'm really sorry you experienced that. Thank you for telling me."*

That moment of acknowledgment builds trust and makes it safer for people to come forward again in the future. Next, get specific. Ask for the details. Dates, times,

---

[52] (Whitson, 2012)

exact words, where it happened, how long it's been going on. Do this with tenderness, you need to get an exact picture, but you don't want it to feel like a cross examination.

Then shift into support mode: *"What do you need right now to take care of yourself and keep doing your job well?"* Sometimes that means a day off. Sometimes it means remote work for a few days. Sometimes it's as simple as not being put on the same project with the person in question. Whatever it is, give them options and let them choose what safety looks like.

Once you've supported the person who brought this forward, it's time to address the person who made the first individual feel bullied. If the person they're reporting isn't one of your direct reports, go to their manager. If they are, then it's time for a one on one.

Don't come in swinging. Open a window and ask, *"How are your working relationships going? I've heard a little bit of drama. What's your take on what's happening?"*

This gives them space to share their view, especially if this is early-stage conflict and not a pattern of aggression. You'll find many people know exactly what you're talking about, and they usually apologize for the action and explain what pressure caused them to say it. What looks like aggression is actually something else. A life crisis. A personal loss. An emotional overflow that's spilling into work. If the person has been kind or neutral in the past, you can usually sense that something has shifted.

When that's the case, say, *"This comment wasn't appropriate. I want to check in—what's going on with you?"*

You might hear something like, "I'm sorry. My mom just got a tough diagnosis, my kid isn't sleeping, and I snapped." That's a human moment. And your follow-up is equally human. *"How do you want to make amends? What would the repair look like?"*

Sometimes people genuinely don't realize they've hurt someone. Especially in cultures with tight-knit teams or casual banter, where the line between joking and jabbing can get fuzzy. What was playful yesterday might land like a gut punch today. It's your job to help clarify that line and teach what's okay.

But if it is bullying, meaning the behavior is repeated and harmful, it's time to swap hats. Now you're in supervisor mode. You should say something like, *"This behavior—[insert specific example]—is not aligned with our organizational values. It must stop immediately. It's not acceptable here."*

Let's be honest. Bullies rarely take this well. And if the behavior continues, document and prepare for an exit strategy. A PIP with a short runway (say, four weeks) is fair. The goal is to protect your team and ensure a healthy culture.

I'll be the first to admit, these conversations are uncomfortable. They make our stomachs flip. They can be emotionally loaded, high-stakes, and awkward as hell. But as a leader, you don't get to opt out. Addressing interpersonal harm is part of the job, and timing matters more than most people realize. The longer you wait between when an issue is raised and when you address it, the more room there is for confusion, resentment, or fear to fester. People start wondering, do they not believe me? Do they not care? Are they protecting the other person? Silence becomes a message of its own, and it's rarely the one you want to send.

That's why I make it a rule to move fast. If someone brings me a concern on a Monday, I try to have the second conversation with the person whose behavior is in question by the end of the week. That gives me time to listen, investigate, and process without dragging my feet. I want my team to see that their safety, dignity, and work environment matter enough to act quickly. We are not going to run a team where snide remarks, character digs, or personality critiques are tolerated. We don't need to like each other's shoes or Spotify playlists, but we do need to treat each other with basic respect.

Now, sometimes the problem is obvious. A cruel comment. A public takedown. A sarcastic jab that cut too deep. But other times? It's sneakier. Especially in upper management, where emotional manipulation can get dressed up as "strategy" or masked by humor. I call this the Jedi mind trick version of bullying. It's subtle, hard to pin down, but still damaging.

As leaders, we need to be vigilant about those dynamics too. A good rule of thumb? If someone is making critical remarks about a colleague's character, not their behavior, not their work product, but who they are, that's a red flag. The only time it's appropriate to bring up someone's personal traits is when you're advocating for yourself or reporting an issue through the proper channels. Otherwise, keep it professional, kind, and clear.

You Won't Always Pick the Right Hat— And That's Okay

By now, you've probably realized that great management is less about having one right approach and more about knowing which version of you the moment needs. That said, here's a quick cheat sheet for some common workplace scenarios:

- An employee is nervous about giving a presentation to leadership → *Coach Hat*
- A new hire is still figuring out how things work → *Mentor Hat*
- You've noticed someone's been unusually quiet in meetings → *Friend Hat*
- An employee asks for more flexibility in their schedule → *Supervisor Hat*
- Rising tension is showing between two teammates → *Leader Hat*
- An employee comes to you and says, "I'm pregnant" (or shares a major life/health update) → *Friend Hat (with a side of Supervisor)*
- A sub-manager reports their direct report is consistently showing up an hour late → *Coach Hat (Mentor Hat if they are new to supervising)*
- Three teammates are dealing with personal drama that's now impacting work → *Leader Hat*
- An employee slams the door twice, and on purpose → *Supervisor Hat*

- An employee is promoted into a different department → *Mentor Hat*
- A recession hits → *Leader Hat (with a strong Friend Hat underneath)*
- The CEO at your company changes → *Leader Hat*
- An employee is storing personal items in shared space → *Supervisor Hat*
- An employee spends corporate money on booze → *Supervisor Hat (with a possible Leader Hat follow-up)*

Each hat serves a different purpose, and knowing when to reach for which one is what makes you a thoughtful, human-centered leader. None of these hats are better than the others. The magic is in learning when to switch them and being intentional about *why*. Just like the emotional tools we've explored earlier in this book—self-awareness, emotional regulation, motivation, values, trauma-awareness, and vulnerability—these hats are here to help you show up with clarity and care. They're not rules. They're not rigid frameworks. They're tools. And you won't use them perfectly. You'll wear the Coach Hat when you should've worn the Supervisor Hat. You'll show up as a Friend when the moment really needs a Leader. You'll miss a cue, misread the room, or bring your own hard day into someone else's moment. That's human. What matters is noticing, learning, and adjusting as you go.

The good news is that with practice, switching between roles becomes more intuitive. You begin to sense when someone needs space to vent versus structure to move forward. Mid-sentence, you may recognize the shift and adjust your approach with ease. And your team? They will notice and trust you more because they see you trying to show up with care, presence, and intention.

Conclusion:
Skip the Perfection

You don't have to be a perfect human to be a good manager. *Read that again.*

Perfect communications skills and a degree in emotional intelligence are not required to be a good manager. You just have to show up, pay attention, and care enough to keep trying, even when it's uncomfortable.

The tools in this book aren't about turning you into some ideal version of a leader. They're about helping you create a more connected work environment. When you build a workplace where people feel respected, seen, and safe, they do better work. And frankly, if we're going to spend this much of our lives at work, it should feel like a place worth being, not something we simply survive.

Your mission and vision depend on this. The future of your organization depends on this. We are shifting out of a culture of company-first loyalty and into an era defined by personal alignment. Gen Z and Gen Alpha aren't giving decades of their lives to places that don't feel good to be in. Unlike the Boomer generation, who put corporate loyalty first, their loyalty is to self and family, to mental health and to meaning. I admire them for that, and I wish I would have had some of their moxie in my earlier career chapters.

Their mindset will challenge Gen X and Millennial managers who were trained to be loyal to organizations, even when those organizations weren't loyal to us. The incoming workforce is gig-based, mobile, and intentional. If the culture feels toxic, Gen Z and Gen Alpha will be gone. No warning. Just a vanishing act worthy of a magician (ghosting has moved beyond dates, my friends). So, as Boomers make their exit from corporate America, and this new generation of managers (Gen X and Millennials) are starting to manage the new workforce (Gen Z and Gen Alpha), the focus will need to be on connection.

This is why I believe the future of leadership isn't about control. I once coached a young man in his early thirties who believed people wouldn't respect him if they saw his humanity. So, he kept his distance. Didn't share anything personal. Thought he had to "earn his stripes" in silence. But I nudged him—just a little—to try opening up, to let his team see a sliver of his real self. And it made a difference. The mood on his team shifted. People seemed more relaxed and more open. He felt lighter, more authentic, and more at home in his role. That's the power of connection. It creates room for people to breathe, and in that space, trust grows. Then with trust comes creativity, collaboration, and the kind of honest problem-solving that makes work enjoyable.

This book was never meant to hand you a one-size-fits-all management system. But it will teach you the minutiae of managing. It's a collection of tools, prompts, and reframes to help you find your own style. Leadership isn't about picking one identity and sticking to it. It's about knowing who you are, what your people need, and navigating that space with honesty and care.

If you're feeling ready to think differently about management, or if you're ready to support your team in showing up more fully as themselves, I'd love to help. I work with managers and teams in one-on-one settings or in group settings. You can find me on LinkedIn. Together, we'll make the workplace feel more like a place where people actually want to be.

Remember, unless you are literally in charge of a neonatal unit, you are not saving babies. So, let's all calm down a little. You don't have to respond perfectly, instantly, or dramatically when an issue arises. You can pause. You can ask a question. You can come back tomorrow. The best managers aren't the ones who know it all. They're the ones who are willing to ask questions, offer guidance, and listen closely.

I know you can do this. You're already doing it just by caring enough to read a book like this. The world doesn't need more polished robotic managers in tailored suits. It needs thoughtful, compassionate, messy humans who are willing to do the work of leadership and know that being in charge means creating space where others can thrive. I believe in your ability to be one of those people, and I hope—aided by the tools in this book—you believe in it too.

About the Author

Dr. Kate Vawter a leadership expert who makes you feel seen, called in, and maybe just a little bit roasted…in the best way. Equal parts seasoned facilitator, sharp academic, and deeply human coach, she's on a mission to help you lead people like actual people so you can build trust, connection, and results without burning yourself out or losing your humanity.

Kate is a proud "Triple Devil," having earned degrees in Marketing (BS), Public Administration (MPA), and a Doctorate in Leadership and Innovation (EdD) from Arizona State University. She designed and taught courses ranging from Introduction to Leadership to Advanced Quantitative Research Methods. Her doctoral research focused on the role of rapport in student success, and that same insight into human connection forms the foundation of her work with teams and organizations today.

As the founder of Ascent Solutions, Kate has delivered leadership workshops to more than 3,000 professionals across the state of Arizona. Her consulting and coaching practice helps organizations grow healthier cultures by putting relationships at the center of how they work. Whether she's working with a new manager navigating their first tough conversation, or a seasoned executive team trying to rebuild trust, Kate brings a blend of strategy, empathy, and straight talk that cuts through the noise and creates momentum.

Her leadership training started long before she ever set foot on a college campus. Kate grew up in a house where the emotional temperature could shift without warning, and part of surviving meant learning to read those shifts before they happened. She spent her early life tracking the emotions and behaviors of the adults around her, learning to scan the room for signs of calm or chaos. That vigilance became one of her greatest superpowers as a facilitator. It's what makes her able to read a room, sense what's really going on beneath the surface, and create a space where people feel safe.

Her early career was shaped by navigating leadership without training or a safety net. That scrappy, self-taught resilience shaped her empathy. She understands what it feels like to be a leader in over your head, to pretend you know what you're doing when you're not sure, and to care deeply even when you're not sure how to say the right thing.

Those experiences are baked into everything she teaches. Kate doesn't believe in cookie-cutter leadership programs. She believes in context, compassion, and finding tools that actually work for your people. She's trauma-informed, systems-literate, and deeply invested in helping managers understand that their ability to lead isn't about knowing everything, it's about showing up with integrity, curiosity, and just enough humor to keep things from getting too precarious.

She believes leadership is an evolving practice, not a destination. That it's okay to not have the perfect words right away, that feedback can be kind and clear. That trust is the currency of collaboration. And that sometimes the best thing you can do for your team is admit you don't have it all figured out.

If you're looking for a step-by-step system to turn your managers into flawless productivity machines, Kate probably isn't the coach for you. But if you're ready to help your people lead with more heart, more clarity, and a little less corporate nonsense, Dr. Kate Vawter is here for it.

You can find her on LinkedIn or her website at https://www.linkedin.com/in/drkatevawter/.

References

(n.d.). From The PEAK Fleet: https://www.thepeakfleet.com/product/peak-values-core-values-card-deck/

(n.d.). From Mr Ed's Circle of Trust: https://www.mredscircleoftrust.com/

(n.d.). From Apollo: https://apolloneuro.com/?tw_source=google&tw_ad id=616764413512&tw_campaign=11588251424&g ad_source=1&gclid=Cj0KCQiA2oW-BhC2ARIsADSIAWqPC3KVHiUv-TKgBPluo0zK6P8rrcRkKm4H2hNLTGjUR54tFitI kyUaAqpjEALw_wcB

(2025). From University of Rochester Medical Center: https://www.urmc.rochester.edu/community-health/patient-care/self-determination-theory

Akpınar, S., & Karadağ, M. G. (2022, September 13). *Is Vitamin D Important in Anxiety or Depression? What Is the Truth?* From National Library of Medicine: https://pmc.ncbi.nlm.nih.gov/articles/PMC9468237/

Arnsten, A., Mazure, C. M., & Sinha, R. (2012, April 1). *Everyday Stress Can Shut Down the Brain's Chief Command Center.* From Scientific American: https://www.scientificamerican.com/article/this-is-your-brain-in-meltdown/

Bardwick, J. M. (1995). *Danger in the Comfort Zone: From Boardroom to Mailroom -- How to Break the Entitlement Habit That's Killing American Business.*

Barrett, L. F. (2018). *How Emotions are Made: The Secret Life of the Brain.* Mariner Books.

Beechly, L. (2022, August 9). *How a People-First Culture Can Drive World-Class Business Outcomes.* From Perceptyx: https://blog.perceptyx.com/how-a-people-first-culture-can-drive-world-class-business-outcomes

Benson, K. (2017, May 4). *Help Your Partner Understand Your Side of the Conflict in 3 Steps.* From Gottman: https://www.gottman.com/blog/help-your-partner-understand-your-side-of-the-conflict-in-3-steps/

Bond, T. (2022, June 16). *Belonging, DEIB, Diversity & Inclusion, Employee Experience.* From Great Place to Work: https://www.greatplacetowork.com/resources/blog/belonging-in-the-workplace-what-does-it-mean-and-why-does-it-matter

Boyatzis, R. E., & McKee, A. (2005). *Resonant Leadership: Renewing Yourself and Connecting with Others Through Mindfulness, Hope, and Compassion.* Harvard Business Review Press.

Broekhof, R., Nordahl, H. M., Tanum, L., & Selvik, S. G. (2023, March 30). *Adverse childhood experiences and their association with substance use disorders in adulthood: A general population study.* From National Library of Medicine: https://pmc.ncbi.nlm.nih.gov/articles/PMC10106480/

Brown, B. (n.d.). From Brene Brown: https://brenebrown.com/videos/anatomy-trust-video/

Daniels, D. (n.d.). *Are You a Thinker or a Feeler?* From The Strive Project: https://magazine.thestriveproject.com/issue/jul-sept-2018/are-you-a-thinker-or-a-feeler/#:~:text=According%20to%20my%20Myers%20Briggs,Thinkers%20and%2060%20percent%20Feelers

Deci, E. L., & Cascio, W. F. (1972, January). *Changes in Intrinsic Motivation as A Function of Negative Feedback and Threats.* From Research Gate: https://www.researchgate.net/publication/234620112_Changes_in_Intrinsic_Motivation_as_A_Function_of_Negative_Feedback_and_Threats

Deci, E. L., & Flaste, R. (1995). *Why we do what we do: The dynamics of personal autonomy.* From Research Gate: https://www.researchgate.net/publication/232484008_Why_we_do_what_we_do_The_dynamics_of_personal_autonomy

Deci, E. L., Nezlek, J., & Sheinman, L. (1981). *Characteristics of the rewarder and intrinsic motivation of the rewardee.* From APA PsycNet: https://psycnet.apa.org/record/1981-33561-001

Does walking for mental health actually improve wellbeing? (n.d.). From Calm.com: https://www.calm.com/blog/walking-for-mental-health

Dweck, C. S. (2007). *Mindset: The New Psychology of Success.* Ballantine Books.

Foo, S. (2023`). *What My Bones Know: A Memoir of Healing from Complex Trauma.* Ballantine Books.

Goleman, D. (2013). *Primal Leadership, With a New Preface by the Authors: Unleashing the Power of Emotional Intelligence.* Harvard Business Review Press.

Gonzales, M. (2022, October 14). From SHRM: https://www.shrm.org/topics-tools/news/all-things-work/belonging-matters-all-things-work

Graham, L. (2008, September 5). *The Neuroscience of Attachment.* From https://lindagraham-mft.net/the-neuroscience-of-attachment/

Guy-Evans, O. (2023). *Amygdala Hijack: How It Works, Signs, & How To Cope.* From Simply Psychology: https://www.simplypsychology.org/amygdala-hijack.html

Guy-Evans, O. (2025). *Amygdala: What It Is & Its Functions.* From Simply Psychology: https://www.simplypsychology.org/amygdala.html

Javanbakht, A., & Saab, L. (2017, October 27). *What Happens in the Brain When We Feel Fear.* From Smithsonian Magazine: https://www.smithsonianmag.com/science-nature/what-happens-brain-feel-fear-180966992/

Jordan, R. (2015, June 5). *Stanford researchers find mental health prescription: Nature.* From Standford Report: https://news.stanford.edu/stories/2015/06/hiking-mental-health-063015

Kent, J. T. (2023, December 5). *Your brain on nature: how exposure to natural environments heals, calms and cures.* From Nevada Today:

https://www.unr.edu/nevada-today/news/2023/atp-nature-and-the-brain

Ledoux, J. (1998). *The Emotional Brain: The Mysterious Underpinnings of Emotional Life.* Simon & Schuster.

Miserandino, C. (2003). *The Spoon Theory.* From https://lymphoma-action.org.uk/sites/default/files/media/documents/2020-05/Spoon%20theory%20by%20Christine%20Miserandino.pdf

Motivational Interviewing Definition Principles Approach. (n.d.). From University of Massachusetts Amherst: https://www.umass.edu/studentlife/sites/default/files/documents/pdf/Motivational_Interviewing_Definition_Principles_Approach.pdf

Quintero, E. (2014, November 20). *Feeling Socially Connected Fuels Intrinsic Motivation And Engagement.* From Albert Shanker Institute: https://www.shankerinstitute.org/blog/feeling-socially-connected-fuels-intrinsic-motivation-and-engagement

Raihan, N., & Cogburn, M. (2022). *Stages of Change Model (Transtheoretical Model).* From Rural Health Information Hub: https://www.ruralhealthinfo.org/toolkits/health-promotion/2/theories-and-models/stages-of-change

Ridenour, E. (2024, January 6). *5 Scientifically Proven Benefits of Morning Sunlight for Sleep-Wake Cycle.* From National Library of Medicine:

https://amerisleep.com/blog/benefits-of-morning-sunlight-for-sleep/

Rock, D. (n.d.). *David Rock's SCARF Model*. From Mindtools: https://www.mindtools.com/akswgc0/david-rocks-scarf-model

Rogers, M. (2022, November 14). *8 ways a walk can help you de-stress*. From Blue Cross NC: https://www.bluecrossnc.com/blog/healthy-living/fitness/benefits-of-walking

Rusnak, K. (2020, December 7). *The Magic Ratio: The Key to Relationship Satisfaction*. From Gottman: https://www.gottman.com/blog/the-magic-ratio-the-key-to-relationship-satisfaction/

Ryan, R., & Wilson, J. H. (2014). Professor-Student Rapport Scale: Psychometric properties of the brief version. *Journal of the Scholarship of Teaching and Learning*.

Scholz, M. (2023, January 31). *Weighted decision matrix: A tool for pro-level prioritization*. From Airfocus: https://airfocus.com/blog/weighted-decision-matrix-prioritization/

Staake, J. (2024, July 5). *What Is Scaffolding in Education?* From We Are Teachers: https://www.weareteachers.com/what-is-scaffolding-in-education/

Using the Diver's Reflex to Regulate Emotional Intensity. (2022, March 6). From Kind Mind Psychology: https://www.kindmindpsych.com/using-the-divers-reflex-to-regulate-emotional-intensity/

Vawter, K. (n.d.). From I'm Glad You Asked Games:
https://imgladyouaskedgames.com/

What ACEs do you have? (n.d.). From ACEs Too High:
https://acestoohigh.com/got-your-ace-score/

Whitson, S. (2012, November 25). *Is It Rude, Is It Mean,
Or Is It Bullying?* From Psychology Today:
https://www.psychologytoday.com/us/blog/passive-
aggressive-diaries/201211/is-it-rude-is-it-mean-or-
is-it-bullying

Xie, H., & al, e. (2017, December 8). *Relationship of
hippocampal volumes and posttraumatic stress
disorder symptoms over early post-trauma periods.*
From National Library of Medicine:
https://pmc.ncbi.nlm.nih.gov/articles/PMC6233727/